Fat Bombs; 100 Sweet & Savory Recipes for the Ketogenic Diet, Paleo Diet and Gluten Free Diet.

Introduction: ketogenic Diet and Fat Bombs

Ketogenic Diet is a low-carbohydrate, high fat and modest protein nutritional plan that uses the process of ketosis to accelerate the rate at which fats are burned by the body.

Typically, when the body requires energy, it will burn sources of carbohydrates first which are turned into glucose and processed throughout the body. This process is particularly helpful with brain function and can be evidenced by the fact that, without a source of quality carbohydrates, we can feel a little sluggish in our mind. With the Ketogenic Diet being low in the principle energy source, the body has to find alternative supplies; this is where the diet part kicks in. Without carbohydrates, the liver looks instead to fat and turns these into fatty acids and Ketone bodies. The brain can use these Ketones as a replacement for glucose and continue to function while the body goes into a state of ketosis. It is in this state that fat is burned at a higher rate.

The Basics of the Ketogenic Diet

Put quite simply, the Ketogenic diet is a high-fat, low carb, moderate protein diet. Got it? Great. Now let's get into the specifics. It is really quite simple. Once you get started on it, you'll find it to be very intuitive.

All human bodies require three main macronutrients to survive: carbohydrates, proteins, and fats. For years, we have been taught that we need to eat a high carb, moderate protein, and low fat diet. But what has that really lead to? High rates of obesity, sickness, and poor health across the board. Eating high carb leads people to go on binges, eating too much, and making themselves sick. What if we change our thinking, and entirely change the focus of our diets?

The Keto diet changes the focus from carbs to fat. On a Keto diet, you want your intake to be very high-fat, with close to zero carbohydrates. Most Keto practitioners eat 80% of their daily calories from fat. So what does that look like?

1 gram of fat has 9 calories. So if you're operating on a 2,000-calorie diet per day, you need 80% of that to come from fat. 80% of 2,000 calories would be 1,600 calories, or 178 grams of fat per day. Don't worry, there isn't this much math involved in day-to-day Keto eating!

Okay, but what about the other two macronutrients? On a Keto diet, you'll eat 80% fat, 15% protein, and only 5% carbs. Let's continue with our 2,000-calorie example. 1 gram of carbohydrates and protein both have 4 calories. On a 2,000-calorie diet, you'll want 15% to be protein, which works out to 300 calories, or 75 grams of protein. Carbs are even less — 5% of your 2,000 calories. That ends up being only 100 calories, or 25 grams of carbohydrates.

So in a typical Keto day, you'll eat 178 grams of fat, 75 grams of protein, and 25 grams of carbohydrates. If you're feeling a bit overwhelmed, don't worry, we're going to do the hard work for you.

At the end of this book, we've included a meal plan and list of meal suggestions so you can easily stay within these guidelines.

The big takeaway is this: on Keto, you get almost all of your daily calories from fats, and reduce your intake of carbohydrates down close to nothing.

Table of Contents

Chapter 1) What are Fat Bombs

Fat bombs are low-protein, low-carb and high-fat snacks. They are good sources of energy to the body and good for those who want to take healthy fats. Fat bombs can be used as snacks before or after a workout.

Fat bombs were initially meant for people who were on a ketogenic diet. A ketogenic diet is a diet taken people who need to lose weight without starving themselves. Fats bombs are a good part of ketogenic diet.

Fat bombs usually feature ingredients such as coconut oil, butter, seeds and nuts. Fat bombs can help you get your body into the process of ketosis, in which you will burn the body fats without starving yourself, and you will shed the extra pounds. Ketogenic fat bombs can be used as a breakfast snack or as a mid-afternoon snack.

Utilizing Fat Bombs

Once you have made the decision to cut almost all of the carbohydrates from your diet, you'll need to come up with additional ways to feel full and gain energy between meals. This is where fat bombs come in; fat bombs are quick and easy to eat snacks that are typically made from a small number of sweet or savory ingredients. Fat bombs can also include foods such as; seeds, nuts, coconut oil and butter, which are the healthy fats that your body is now relying upon.

These concentrated energy snacks will quickly fill you up and prevent you from breaking down during the day. But, best of all, fat bombs are so tasty that you will never feel tempted to reach for something that's been processed and packed full of carbohydrates. Fat bombs are a great choice before the gym or when you are struggling to make it from lunch all the way to dinner. Plus, getting the required amount of fat in your diet every day can be more difficult than it first appears. Remember, it is important to always stick to healthy fats otherwise you are just binging on items that have little true nutritional value.

Fat Bomb precautions: Like any other new dietary supplement, when you first begin trying out different fat bomb recipes it is important to do so cautiously at first as you never know how your body might respond. As previously discussed, it's likely that your body hasn't regularly consumed this much healthy fat before, it may take a little while to accept the change. However, if you keep at it you should find that you have adapted to the change relatively quickly. It is important to consume fat bombs in moderation as relying on them too heavily can cause a dependence to form. They should be a small part of your daily ketogenic diet, not a core pillar. Use discretion if you find yourself eating more than 2 per day.

Fat bomb creation basics: Yes, this is a cookbook that contains 250 fat bomb recipes, so you may not care too much about creating your own unique fat bombs. However, if you do which to understand the process behind the creation of the fat bomb, read this short section mentioned below...

Fat bombs are a great addition to a low carbohydrate and protein diet as they are typically based either around satisfying cravings you might have for either sweet or savory foods. What's more, they are infinitely malleable as the only requirement is lots of healthy fats, the rest is up for you.

When it comes to making your own fat bomb recipes, it is important to shoot for an item that is high in fat, this will ensure your bombs are as effective as possible. Typically, fat bombs contain only a few ingredients, generally they start with a base of healthy fat, typically a coconut derivative, grass-fed butter or cream cheese, still other fat bombs can vary. Some type of flavoring and an additional ingredient or two is usually added to the fat bomb.

As a rule, coconut oil is the healthiest option when it comes to choosing a base fat. It is the type of fat that burns the quickest, and, once your body reaches ketosis, it is turned into energy practically as soon as it is absorbed by your body.

Chapter 2) Sweet Fat Bomb recipes:

Delight Coconut and Cinnamon Muffin

Prep Time: 5 Minutes

Cook Time: 15 Minutes

Serves: 12

Ingredients:

- 1 cup almond flour •

2 tablespoons coconut flour •

1/2 teaspoon baking powder

- 1/4 teaspoon cinnamon

- 1/2 teaspoon salt

- 1/2 cup Swerve / erythritol
- 2 large eggs
- 4 tablespoons coconut oil
- 1/2 teaspoon vanilla extract
- 1/2 teaspoon almond extract
- 1 tablespoon shredded coconut, organic

Directions:

Preheat oven at 355 degrees.

In a bowl add all ingredients and mix well until even.

Transfer into baking dish and bake for 15 minutes. Cut into bars Serve and enjoy.

Nutritional Information
Calories 103
Total Fat: 9.7 g;
Carbohydrates: 3.0 g;
Protein: 2.8 g;

Vanilla Nut Mixed Butter

Prep Time: 5 Minutes

Total Time: 5 Minutes

Serves: 10

Ingredients:

- 2 Cups Macadamia Nuts

- 8-10 Brazil Nuts

- ½ Teaspoon Vanilla Extract

- ¼ Teaspoon Salt

Directions:

1.   Start by placing your Brazil nuts, vanilla, macadamias, and salt in a food processor, and start to blend.

2.   Blend until you get your desired consistency. It'll take about two to four minutes depending on how smooth you want it.

You can store at room temperature for about a week, but you can always store it in the fridge for a month.

Nutritional Information:
Calories: 225
Total Fat: 23.6 g
Total Carbs: 4.3 g
Protein: 2.8 g

Tasty Shredded Coconut Raspberry Fat Bombs

Prep Time: 5 Minutes

Total Time: 25-30 Minutes

Serves: 12

Ingredients:

- ½ Cup Coconut Butter

- ½ Cup Coconut Oil

- ½ Cup Raspberries, Freeze Dried

- ½ Cup Shredded Coconut, Unsweetened

- ¼ Cup Powdered Sugar Substitute (can be Swerve)

Directions:

1.	Take your food processor, and pulse your raspberries until they turn into a fine powder.

2.	Combine your coconut oil, coconut butter, shredded coconut, and sweetener in a saucepan, cooking over medium heat and stirring until fully melted.

3.	Stir in your raspberry powder after you remove it from heat, and then pour it into your molds. 4. Keep it refrigerated until it's solid.

Nutritional Information:
Calories: 169
Total Fat: 18 g
Total Carbs: 3.2 g
Protein: 0.3 g

Healthy Chocolate Layered Coconut Bars

Total Cooking &Prep Time: 30

1 Hour Freezing

Serves: 12

Ingredients:

For the coconut bottom layer:

- 2 cups shredded coconut, unsweetened

- 2 drops liquid stevia

- 1/3 cup coconut oil, virgin, melted For the chocolate top layer:

- 3 squares Baker's chocolate, unsweetened (1 Baker's unsweetened chocolate bar is 1 ounce)

- 2 drops liquid stevia (about 1 teaspoon stevia powder)

- 1 tablespoon coconut oil

Directions:

For the coconut bottom layer:

1.Into a food processor, using the S-blade, place the entire ingredients.

2.Process until the mixture forms into dough that falls away from the sides. Scrape down the sides when needed.

3.When sufficiently processed, put the mixture into the bottom of a 9×5-inches silicone loaf pan. For a thinner layer, use an 8×8-inches silicone cake pan.

4.Place the pan in the freezer while preparing the chocolate top layer.

For the chocolate top layer:

1.Put the chocolate and the coconut oil in a microwavable bowl. At 50% power, microwave the mixture until the oil and chocolate has melted.

2.When melted, remove bowl from the microwave. Add the sweetener and mix the ingredients until smooth.

3.Pour the melted chocolate over the frozen coconut layer, spreading evenly. Return to the freezer and freeze for about 30 minutes or until the layers are frozen together.

4.When frozen, turn the pan inside out, releasing the frozen mixtures.

5.Cut into 12 equal-sized bars.

Storage:

Place in a Ziploc and keep in the freezer.

Nutritional Information:
Calories: 145
Total Fat: 15.3 g;
Carbohydrates: 5.2 g;
Protein: 1.4 g;

Great Treat Coconut Candy

Prep Time: 5 Minutes

Total Time: 15 Minutes

Serves: 10

- ⅓ Cup Coconut Butter, Softened

- ⅓ Cup Coconut Oil, Melted

Ingredients:

- 1 Ounce Shredded Coconut, Unsweetened - 1 Teaspoon Sugar

Substitute

Directions:

1. Start by mixing all of your ingredients together, and make sure that the sugar substitute is well dissolved.
2. Pour into silicone molds, and then refrigerate for about an hour.

Nutritional Information:

Calories: 104
Total Fat: 11 g
Total Carbs: 0.8 g
Protein: 0.3 g

Cocoa Minty Chocolate Fat Bombs

Prep Time: 10 Minutes

Total Time: 20 Minutes

Serves: 6

Dairy Free, Nut Free

Ingredients:

- ½ Cup Coconut Oil, Melted

- 2 Tablespoons Cocoa Powder

- 1 Tablespoon Granulated Stevia (or sweetener of choice)

- ½ Teaspoon Peppermint Essence

Directions:

1.   Start by melting your coconut oil, and adding your peppermint essence and sweetener.

2.   Add cocoa powder to half of the mixture and mix well in another bowl.

3.   Pour the chocolate mixture into the silicone molds, and then place them in the fridge. Refrigerate for 5-10 minutes.

3.   Make the mint layer by pouring the mint mixture into the silicon molds. Refrigerate for another 5-10 minutes.

4.   Pour the last layer of chocolate mixture into the molds. Refrigerate and let harden.

Nutritional Information:
Calories: 161
Total Fat: 18.5 grams
Total Carbs: 1.15 g
Protein: 0.4 grams

Vanilla Coconut Almond Bars

Prep Time: 15 Minutes

Cooking Time: 10 Minutes

4 Hours Freezing

Serves: 24

Ingredients:

- 1/2 cup cocoa butter, melted • 1/4 cup pistachio nuts, chopped • 1 cup coconut butter

- 1 cup almond butter

- 1 cup coconut oil, firm

- 1 teaspoon coconut milk, chilled

- 1 tablespoon vanilla extract

- 1/4 teaspoon almond extract

- 1/4 cup ghee

- 2 teaspoons Chai spice

- 1/4 teaspoon sea salt

Directions:

1.Grease a 9-inch baking pan and then line it with parchment paper. Set aside.

2.In a small saucepan over low heat, melt the cocoa butter, stirring often. Set aside.

3.Except for the pistachios and cocoa butter, put the rest of the ingredients into a large mixing bowl. With a hand mixer on low speed, mix the ingredients, increasing to high speed, until everything is well-blended, airy, and light.

4.Pour the melted cocoa butter into the mixture. On low speed, continue mixing for about 1-2 minutes.

5.Transfer the mixture into the prepared baking pan. Spread it as evenly as possible.

6.Sprinkle the chopped pistachios over. Refrigerate for about 4-5 hours or until completely set. Freezing it overnight is best.

7.When frozen, cut into 24 equal-sized pieces.

Nutritional Information:
Calories: 227
Total Fat: 23.5 g;
Carbohydrates: 3.2 g;
Protein: 2.6 g;

Mini Strawberry Cheesecake

Prep Time: 5 Minutes

Total Time: 15-20 Minutes

Serves: 8

Ingredients:
- ½ Cup Strawberries, Fresh & Mashed

- ¾ Cup Cream Cheese, Softened

- ¼ Cup Coconut Oil, Softened

- 10-15 Drops Liquid Stevia

- 1 Teaspoon Vanilla Extract

Directions:

1.   Start by combining all of the ingredients in a bowl, and mixing with a hand mixer until completely smooth. You can also do this in a high-speed blender.

2.   Spoon into mini muffin tins, and place in the freezer. It'll take about two hours to set, and then you can place them in the fridge.

Nutritional Information:
Calories: 129
Total Fat: 13.27 g
Protein: 1.66 g
Total Carbs: 1.55 g

Low-Carb Almond Balls

Prep Time: 15 Minutes

Freeze For: 15 Minutes

Serves: 4

Ingredients:
• 2 tablespoons almond butter

- 2 tablespoons coconut oil, melted

- 2 tablespoons cocoa powder

- 1 tablespoon coconut flour

- Splenda, to taste (or equivalent low-carb sweetener)

Directions:

1. Mix the coconut oil and the cocoa powder.

2. Add the almond butter.

3. Mix until smooth.

4. Add the coconut flour and the sweetener.

5. Form into balls.

6. Place the mixture on wax paper.

7. Freeze for about 5 minutes.

Nutritional Information:
Calories: 128
Total Fat: 12.8 g;
Carbohydrates: 3.7 g;
Protein: 2.3 g;

Stevia Lemon Bombs

Prep Time: 5-10 Minutes

Total Time: 35-45 Minutes

Serves: 16

Ingredients:

- ¾ Cup Coconut Butter, Softened

- ¼ Cup Virgin Coconut Oil, Softened

- 2 Tablespoons Lemon Extract

- ¼ Tablespoon Lemon Zest - 15-20 Drops Stevia Extract

Directions:

1.   Start by mixing your coconut butter and coconut oil until blended.

2.   Add lemon extract, lemon zest and liquid sweetener and stir. Make sure that it's completely blended.

3.   Take mini muffin paper cups, and put a tablespoon of the mixture in each one before placing them in the fridge.

4.   Refrigerate them until they're solid. This can take anywhere from thirty minutes to an hour depending on where you place them and what temperature your fridge is set at. Pop one out when you want to eat it.

Nutritional Information:
Calories: 118; Total Fat: 13.6 g Carbs: 0.15 g ;Protein: 0.01 g

Coconut Ginger Bombs
Prep Time: 5 Minutes

Total Time: 20 Minutes

Serves: 10

Ingredients:

- ⅓ Cup Coconut Butter, Softened

- ⅓ Cup Coconut Oil, Softened

- 2 Tablespoons Shredded Coconut, Unsweetened

- 1 Teaspoon Powdered Sweetener - 1 Teaspoon Ginger Powder

Directions:

1. Mix all of your ingredients, and then pour them into a jug. Make sure that you dissolve the sweetener.

2. Once it's dissolved, pour the mixture in silicon molds, and then refrigerate for at least 10 minutes.

Nutritional Information:
Calories: 120
Total Fat: 12.8 g
Protein: 0.5 g
Total Carbs: 2.2 g

Sugar Free Vanilla Lemon

Prep Time: 15 Minutes

Freezing Time: 30 Minutes

Serves: 12

Ingredients:
- 1/2 cup coconut butter, softened

- 1/2 cup coconut oil, extra-virgin, softened

- Juice and zest of 1 lemon
- Seeds from 1/2 of a vanilla bean

Directions:

1.Into a spouted cup, whisk all of the ingredients together.

For discs:

1.Line a 12-mold mini cupcake pan with parchment paper liners.

2.Pour the coconut butter mixture into the liners, dividing evenly.

3.Refrigerate for about 30 minutes or until the mixture is firm.

4.If desired, garnish with fresh lemon zest.

For mini cubes:

1.Line a loaf pan with parchment paper.

2.Pour the coconut butter into the pan.

3.Refrigerate for about 30 minutes or until the mixture is firm.

4.Cut into 1/2-inch cubes. Plate them with toothpicks.

5.If desired, garnish with fresh lemon zest.

Nutritional Information:
Calories: 105 ;Total Fat: 11.3 g;
;Carbohydrates: 1.5 g; ;Protein: 0.3 g;

Peanut Butter Chocolate Cups

Prep Time: 15 Minutes

Cook Time: 10 Minutes

Freezing Time: 30 Minutes

Serves: 12

Ingredients:

- 3/4 cup coconut oil

- 1/4 cup cocoa powder

- 1/4 cup peanut butter

- 1 teaspoon coconut oil

- 30 drops liquid stevia, to taste

Directions:

1.Heat the 3/4 cup coconut oil until melted. When melted, divide into 3 bowls.

2.In one bowl of oil, stir in the cocoa powder until completely dissolved. Add about 6 drops of liquid stevia. Stir to mix.

3.In another bowl of oil, add the peanut butter. Blend until smooth. Add 6 drops of liquid stevia.

4.In the last bowl, add the 1 teaspoon coconut oil. Add the remaining liquid stevia.

5.Divide the chocolate mixture into 12 small cups. Refrigerate for about 10 minutes or until firm.

6.When chocolate mix is firm, divide the peanut butter mixture over the chocolate mixture. Return to the fridge until set. When firm, divide the coconut oil mixture over the hard peanut butter layer. Chill until firm and ready to serve.

Nutritional Info :
Calories: 153 ;Total Fat: 16.6 g;
;Carbohydrates: 2.1 g; ;Protein: 1.7 g;

Healthy Chocolate & Cayenne Bombs

Prep Time: 5 Times

Total Time: 15 Minutes

Serves: 12

Ingredients:

- ¼ Cup Coconut Oil

- ¼ Cup Salted Butter, Melted

- ¼ Cup Almond Butter

- 2 Tablespoons Cocoa Powder

- 3 Teaspoons Liquid Sweetener

- ¼ Teaspoon Cayenne Pepper

Directions:

1. Melt coconut oil and butter in a saucepan over low heat.

2. Mix all of your ingredients together in a mixing bowl, and then pour them into silicon molds of your choice.

2. Freeze for at least 30 minutes before eating.

Nutritional Information:

Total Carbs: 2.85 g
Protein: 1.42 g
Total Fat: 10.14 g
Calories: 102

Copycat Sugar-Free Ferrero Rocher

Prep Time: 10 Minutes

Freezing Time: 1-2 Hours

Serves: 12

Ingredients:

For the balls:

• 1/2 cup homemade Nutella, recipe follows in Other Ketogenic Desserts • 12 hazelnuts

For the coating:

• 2 ounces chocolate bar, sugar-free • 1/4 cup hazelnuts, chopped

Directions:

1.In a dry skillet, toast the hazelnuts until fragrant. When toasted, remove as much skin as possible. Allow to cool.

2.Refrigerate the homemade Nutella for about 30 minutes. Scoop 1 teaspoon of Nutella, flatten like a mini pancake, and place in a parchment lined baking sheet.

3.Top the flattened Nutella with 1 hazelnut. Top with another 1 teaspoon flattened Nutella. Mold into ball shape. Make 12 balls. Refrigerate.

4.Melt the chocolate bar. When melted, stir in the chopped nuts. Mix well.

5.Line a baking sheet with parchment paper. Place a wire rack on the baking sheet.

6.Take 1 Nutella ball. Hold the ball with fork, dip in the chocolate coating, and take out, removing excess. Place the coated balls in the prepared wire rack. Repeat with the remaining ingredients.

7.Refrigerate until the coating is hard.

8.Individually wrap each ball with foil, if desired. Store in an airtight container and keep refrigerated until ready to serve.

Nutritional Information:
Calories: 161
Total Fat: 15.8 g;
Carbohydrates: 5.4 g;
Protein: 3.9 g;

Nutmeg Cinnamon Coconut Balls

Prep Time: 90 Minutes

Cook Time: 5 Minutes

Serves: 10

Ingredients:
• 1 cup coconut butter (or almond butter)

• 1 cup coconut milk (canned, full fat)

• 1 cup coconut, shredded

• 1 teaspoon stevia powder extract (or to taste)

• 1 teaspoon vanilla extract (gluten-free)

• 1/2 teaspoon cinnamon

• 1/2 teaspoon nutmeg

Directions:

1.Put a few inches of water into a saucepan. Place a glass bowl over, creating a double boiler.

2.Except for the shredded coconut, put all of the ingredients into the bowl. Heat over medium heat, mixing the ingredients until melted. Combine well.

3.Place the bowl in the fridge, cooling the mixture for about 30 minutes until it's hard enough to roll into balls.

4.Roll into 1-inch ball and then roll into shredded coconut.

5.Place the balls on a plate and then refrigerate for about 1 hour.

6.Keep refrigerated.

Nutritional Information:
Calories: 142 ;Total Fat: 13.8 g;Carbohydrates: 5.3 g; ;Protein: 1.4 g;

Craving Icy Mocha Fat Bombs

Prep Time: 10 Minutes

Total Time: 1 Hour 10 Minutes

Serves: 12

Ingredients:
- 8.5 Ounces Cream Cheese

- 2 Tablespoons Powdered Sweetener

- 2 Tablespoons Cocoa Powder, Unsweetened

- ¼ Cup Strong Coffee, Chilled

- 2.5 Ounces Dark Chocolate, Melted - 1 Ounce Cocoa Butter,

  Melted

Directions:

1. Start by adding your coffee, cream cheese, cocoa powder, and sweetener in a blender, and pulse until it's completely smooth.

2. Roll about two tablespoons of the mixture into small bowls, putting them on a baking sheet lined with parchment paper. This recipe should make twelve.

3. Now, blend the melted dark chocolate and cocoa butter until smooth.

4. Roll your balls in the chocolate coating and place them back on the tray.

5. Freeze them for 1 hour or until set.

Nutritional Info:

Carbs: 6.52 g ;Protein: 2.4 g ;Fat: 9.9 grams ;Calories: 120

Walnut Vanilla Crème Parfaits

Prep Time: 10 Minutes

Serves: 4

Ingredients:

• 1 can (398 ml) coconut milk, full-fat, chilled • 10 drops liquid stevia (or 1 packet stevia powder) • 1 teaspoon vanilla extract, pure, alcohol-free preferred • 6 ounces berries, fresh • 3 ounces walnuts, chopped Optional:

Ground cinnamon

Directions:

1. In the bowl of a stand mixer, add the coconut milk, vanilla extract, and stevia. Whip with the whisk attachment for about 30 seconds until well-mixed. Set aside.

2. In a large bowl, mix the walnuts and the berries. Set aside.

3. Put about 3 spoonfuls of vanilla-coconut crème pudding into 4 jars. Divide 1/2 of the walnut mix between the 4 jars. Spoon a second layer of the vanilla crème pudding over the walnut mixture. Add the remaining walnut mix.

4. Sprinkle each jar with ground cinnamon, if desired.

Nutritional Information:
Calories: 399
Total Fat: 37.5 g;
Carbohydrates: 13.6 g
Protein: 8 g;

Delicious Lime Avocado Vanilla Pudding

Prep Time: 15 Minutes

Serves: 4

Ingredients:
• 1 can (13.5 fl. ounce or 400 ml) coconut milk, organic

• 1 tablespoon lime juice, freshly squeezed

- 2 Hass avocados, ripe, peeled, pitted and cut into chunks

- 2 teaspoons vanilla extract

- ¾ teaspoon of liquid stevia (or 8 packets stevia powder)

Directions:

1.Put all of the ingredients into the blender. Close the blender lid.

2.Blend until velvety smooth.

Nutritional Information:
Calories: 445
Total Fat: 43.8 g;
Carbohydrates: 18.8 g;
Protein: 4.2 g;

Delight Vanilla Cheesecake Fat Bombs
Prep Time: 5 Minutes

Total Time: 15 Minutes

Serves: 8

Ingredients:
- 6 Ounces Cream Cheese, Softened

- ½ Cup Heavy Whipping Cream

- 1 ½ Teaspoons Vanilla Extract

- ¼ Cup Erythritol or Other Sugar Substitute

- ¼ Teaspoon Salt

Directions:

1. Add cream cheese, sugar substitute, salt and vanilla extract to a blender. Blend it until smooth.

2. Slowly add the heavy cream.

3. Continue to blend until it's thickened, which will take one to two minutes. It should have a mousse like consistency once you're done.

4. Spoon the mixture into a piping bag and pipe into 8 mini cupcake liners. Chill for one hour until they are set. Keep them refrigerated.

Nutritional Information:
Total Carbs: 1.05 g
Protein: 1.66 g
Total Fat: 8.86 g
Calories: 91

Favorite Coconut Pudding

Prep Time: 15 Minutes

Total Time: 15 Minutes

Serves: 4

Ingredients:
• 1 2/3 cups coconut milk • 1 tablespoon gelatin

• 1/2 teaspoon vanilla extract

- 3 egg yolks

- 3 tablespoons honey (or ½ teaspoon liquid stevia)

Directions:

1. In a small bowl, pour the gelatin and 1 tablespoon of the coconut milk. Set aside.

2. In a medium saucepan over medium-low heat, pour the remaining coconut milk and the honey/sweetener.

3. Cook for about 3-5 minutes, stirring occasionally, until the mixture is hot.

4. In a medium bowl, whisking constantly, slowly pour about 1 ladle of the hot milk, add egg yolks.

5. Continuously stirring, pour the egg yolk mixture back into the saucepan.

6. Cook for another 3-4 minutes, or until the mixture is slightly thicker.

7. Add the gelatin mixture into the pot. Whisk to blend well.

8. Pour the mixture into 4 ramekins.

9. Refrigerate for about 2 hours or until the mixture is set.

Nutritional Information:
Calories: 278
Total Fat: 27.2 g;
Carbohydrates: 9.1 g;
Protein: 5.8 g;

Flavor Matcha Latte Fat Bomb

Prep Time: 5 Minutes

Total Time: 10-15 Minutes

Serves: 1

Ingredients:

- ½ Cup Boiling Water

- 1 Teaspoon Matcha Powder

- ⅓ Cup Unsweetened Coconut Milk

- 1 Tablespoon MCT Oil (you can also use extra virgin coconut oil) -

  3 Drops Liquid Stevia

Directions:

1. Start by mixing the matcha powder in the boiling water. Make sure it's completely combined.

2. Add MTC oil and whisk it all over again.

3. Use a milk frother to make the coconut milk froth. Next, pour the froth into the glass with your matcha, and sprinkle matcha powder on top.

4. Add the sweetener before serving. (Optional)

Nutritional Information
Total Carbs: 6.29 grams
Protein: 1.8 grams
Total Fat: 202.5 grams
Calories: 211

Almond Coconut Cookies

Prep Time: 5 Minutes

Total Time: 15 Minutes

Serves:8

Ingredients:
• 1 cup almond flour • 2 eggs

• 1 cup coconut powder • ½ teaspoon vanilla extract • ¼ cup butter

• ½ cup cream milk

Directions:

1.Preheat oven to 355 degrees.

2.In a bowl add eggs and beat until smooth.

3.Add butter, almond flour, coconut powder, cream milk, vanilla extract and beat for 1 minute.

4.Transfer into baking dish and bake for 15 minutes.

5.Serve and enjoy.

Nutritional Information:
Calories: 285
Total Fat: 26.2 g;
Carbohydrates: 8.7 g;
Protein: 7.3 g;

Bacon Cheeseburger Bombs
Make these bombs for your children and they will love them.

Makes: 10 servings Prep Time: 20 min

Ingredients

1 can of Pillsbury Biscuits (10 biscuits)

1 pound of lean ground beef

½ finely chopped onion

3 slices of chopped bacon

⅓ Cup of cream cheese

1 tablespoon of ketchup

2 tablespoons of barbecue sauce

1 teaspoon of yellow mustard

1 teaspoon Worcestershire sauce

5 oz. of cheddar cheese

1 egg white Sesame seeds

Directions

1. Preheat the oven up to 375 degrees.
2. In some large pan, brown bacon, ground beef and the onion until well cooked, then drain any grease.

3. Add cream ketchup, barbecue sauce, cheese, mustard and the Worcestershire sauce.
4. Stir over low heat until the cream cheese melts. Allow these to cool.

5. *Roll every biscuit very thin. Put 2 tablespoons of beef mixture on every biscuit then add 1 square cheese.*

Wrap your biscuit round beef/cheese then tightly seal edges.

6. *Put your biscuits on a pan lined with parchment then seam side down. Brush using egg white then sprinkle with the sesame seeds.*
7. Place them in an oven then turn down heat up to 350 degrees.
8. You can then bake for 13-16 minutes or till lightly browned.
9. Serve when warm.

Nutritional information per serving:

Total carbs 2.3g, Fiber 06g, Protein 3.6g, Fat 34.6g, Magnesium 15mg, Potassium 94mg

Butter Lemon Coconut Cookies

Prep Time: 10 Minutes

Cook Time: 10 Minutes

Serves: 12

Ingredients:
• 3/4 cup coconut butter, softened

- 2/3 – ¾ cup Swerve / erythritol

- 1/4 cup cashew butter (I prefer fresh ground, jarred has added oils)

- 1 teaspoon baking powder (gluten and corn free)

- 1 tablespoon grated lemon peel

- 1 egg

- 1/4 cup FRESH lemon juice, strained (about 1 lemon)

- Dash of sea salt

Directions:

1.Place the softened coconut butter into a blender and food processor. Pulse until the mixture is smooth.

2.Add in the remaining ingredients. Process until well-combined without a trace of lemon peel in the mixture.

3.If your mixture is too soft to mold, refrigerate it for a few minutes to harden.

4.Roll the mixture into 1-inch balls. Place the balls in a parchment lined cookie sheet. Lightly press on the balls to flatten them.

5.Bake at 350F for about 10-12 minutes or until the edges of the cookies are slightly brown.

6.Allow the cookies to cool in the cookie sheet for a few minutes and then transfer on a cooling rack.

7.Store the cookies in an airtight container. If you want harder cookies, then keep in the refrigerator.

Note:

To make your own coconut butter, blend shredded coconut for about 20 minutes or until you make a paste. You can season the butter with salt, if desired.

Nutritional Information:
Calories: 76
Total Fat: 6.7 g;
Carbohydrates: 5.5 g;
Protein: 2.0 g;

Nutmeg Chia Ginger Cookies

Prep Time: 10 Minutes

Cook Time: 15 Minutes

Serves: 12

Ingredients:

• 1 egg

• 1/2 teaspoon nutmeg

- 1/4 cup coconut oil

- 2 cups whole almonds

- 2 tablespoons chia seeds

- 2 tablespoons cinnamon powder

- 3 tablespoons ginger, freshly grated

- Dash of salt

- ¾ teaspoon liquid stevia

Directions:

1.Preheat the oven to 350F or 175C.

2.Blend or food process the chia seeds and the almonds.

3.In a large mixing bowl, mix all the ingredients together.

4.Form into small cookies in a parchment paper lined baking tray.

5.Bake for about 15 minutes at 350F.

Nutritional Information:
Calories: 148 ;Fat: 12.9 g;
Carbohydrates: 6.3 g; Protein: 5.0 g;

Yummy Peanut Butter Balls

Prep Time: 5 Minutes

Freezing Time: 1 Hour

Serves: 8

Ingredients:

- ¼ Cup Peanut Butter

- 2 Tablespoons Butter

- 1 Tablespoon Coconut Oil

- ¼ Cup Peanuts, Crushed

- 3 Drops Liquid Sweetener

Directions:

1. Melt butter, coconut oil and peanut butter in a saucepan over low heat, stirring until combined.

2. Add in your sweetener, and continue to stir.

3. Place the mixture into the freezer for 10 minutes.

3. Form mixture into balls, and then roll them in crushed peanuts.

4. Let chill for at least one hour before serving.

Nutritional Information:
Total Carbs: 2.66 g
Protein: 3.18 g
Total Fat: 9.95 g
Calories: 107

Butter Turmeric Ginger Cookies

Prep Time: 15 Minutes

Cook Time: 10-15 Minutes

Serves: 15

Ingredients:

- 1 cup coconut butter, softened

- 1 egg

- 1 teaspoon turmeric powder

- 1 teaspoon vanilla extract

- 1/4 cup low-carb granulated sweetener

- 1/4 teaspoon baking soda

- 1/4 teaspoon sea salt

- 1/8 teaspoon black pepper, or more

- 2 heaping teaspoons ginger, ground

Directions:

1.Place the egg, coconut butter, and vanilla extract into a food processor. Blend until well-combined.

2.Add the baking soda, sweetener, and all of the spices. Blend again until combined.

3.Form the cookie mixture into 1-inch balls. Place 1 inch apart on a parchment lined cookie sheet. Press each cookie to flatten into cookie shapes. Do not spread too much.

4.Bake at 350F for about 10-15 minutes or until slightly brown.

5.Allow the cookies to cool down a bit on the cookie sheet. They will be fragile fresh out of the oven. When slightly cool, transfer on a cooling rack and allow to cool completely, hardening as they cool.

6.Store in an airtight container.

Notes:

Do not melt the coconut butter completely, just soften it. If the cookie dough mixture does not form into a ball because the butter is too runny, place the mixture in the fridge for a few minutes to make it moldable.

Nutritional Information:
Calories: 44
Total Fat: 3.9 g;
Carbohydrates: 3.6 g;
Protein: 0.8 g;

Quick & Simple Cranberry Fat Bombs

Prep Time: 5 Minutes

Total Time: 15-20 Minutes

Serves: 6

Ingredients:
- 2/3 Cup Cranberries, Dried

- 6 Ounces mascarpone Cheese, Softened

Directions:
1. Chop your cranberries. Make sure that they're chopped fine.

2. Soften your mascarpone cheese, and then blend all ingredients together.

3. Gently spoon the mixture into mini muffin liners and chill for about an hour in the refrigerator before serving.

Nutritional Information:
Total Carbs: 3 g
Protein: 7 g
Total Fat: 10 g
Calories: 125

Chapter 3) Savoury Fat Bomb Recipes :

Delicious Garlic Skillet Pepperoni Pizza

Prep Time: 10 Minutes

Freezing Time: 20 Minutes

Serves: 4

Ingredients:

- 4 ounces mozzarella cheese, or more to cover the bottom of 10inch skillet

- 12 pepperoni slices

- 1 ounce parmesan cheese

- 2 tablespoons tomatoes, crushed

- 1 teaspoon garlic powder

- 1 teaspoon Italian seasoning or dried basil

- 1 teaspoon red pepper, crushed

- 1 teaspoon basil, fresh, torn

Directions:

1.Heat a small, non-stick skillet over medium heat.

2.Evenly cover the bottom with the mozzarella cheese. This will serve as the crust.

3.With the back of a spoon, lightly spread the tomatoes over the cheese, leaving a border around the edges of the cheese crust.

4.Sprinkle with the garlic powder and the Italian seasoning or dried basil.

5.Arrange the pepperoni on top. Cook until bubbled, sizzling, and the edges of the crust are brown.

6.With a spatula, try lifting the edges. When done, the pizza will lift easily from the pan. If the pizza still sticks, it means it is not yet done. Lift and check frequently.

7.When the pizza lifts up easily, work the spatula slowly and gently underneath, loosening up the entire pizza. Transfer to a cutting board.

8.Lightly sprinkle with parmesan, basil leaves, and red pepper.

9.Cool for about 5 minutes to cool and allow the crust to firm. Cut with a pizza cutter. Transfer to a serving plate.

Nutritional Information:
Calories: 196
Total Fat: 14.3 g;
Carbohydrates: 2.8 g;
Protein: 14.5 g;

Keto Sausage Balls

Total Time: 20 Minutes

Serves: 1

Ingredients
1 lb. Breakfast Sausage
1 Large Egg
1 Cup Almond Flour
8 Oz Cheddar Cheese
1/4 Cup Grated Parmesan

1 Tbsp Butter (or Coconut Oil)
2 tsp Baking Powder
1/4 tsp Salt

Directions:

Preheat oven to 350. Add all ingredients in a large mixing bowl and mix until well combined.

Using a cookie scoop and your hands roll sausage mixture into 20-25 sausage balls .Place sausage balls on a cookie sheet Bake for 16-20 minutes. Store in a sandwich bag or covered bowl in the fridge.

Nutritional Information:
Calories: 124
Total Fat: 11g
Carbohydrates: 1g Protein:
6g

Chives Tomato Cheesy Bites

Prep Time: 5-10 Minutes

Cook Time: 15-20 Minutes

Serves: 12

Ingredients:

- 3 Ounces Full Fat Cream Cheese

- 12 Cherry Tomatoes

- ¼ Cup Fresh Chives

- Salt to Taste

Directions:

1. Cut a small slice off the top of each cherry tomato and discard seeds and juice.

2. Chop your chives thin, and then mix it with your softened cream cheese and salt.

3. Fill each tomato with flavored cream cheese.

Nutritional Information:
Total Carbs: 1.03 g
Protein: 0.83 g
Total Fat: 2.74 g
Calories: 31

Yummy Bacon & Green Onions

Prep Time: 5 Minutes

Total Time: 15 Minutes

Serves: 5

Ingredients:
- 5 Strips Bacon

- 6 Green Onions, Trimmed

- 4 Tablespoons Coconut Oil - Salt and Pepper to Taste

Directions:

1. Start by wrapping green onions together using a single strip of bacon. Repeat until all of your bacon and green onions are used.

2. Season

3. Use a frying skillet and heat up coconut oil over medium high heat, frying your wraps until they're slightly browned. This usually takes six to eight minutes.

Nutritional Information:
Total Carbs: 2.82 g
Protein: 1 g
Total Fat: 12.5 g
Calories: 121

Garlic Butter Bacon & Pecan Rolls

Prep Time: 5 Minutes

Total Time: 15 Minutes

Serves: 12

Ingredients:
- 4 Bacon Slices, Cooked

- ½ Cup Pecan Halves, Chopped

- ½ Cup Organic Butter

- 1 Teaspoon Garlic Powder

Directions:

1. Divide your bacon into three parts, and then spread each part with butter.

2. Press your pecan pieces into the butter.

3. Sprinkle with garlic and roll up.

Nutritional Information:
Total Carbs: 0.83 g
Protein: 1.53 g
Total Fat: 14.87 g
Calories: 139

Cheddar Scallions Creamy Bacon Dip

Prep Time: 5-10 Minutes

Total Time: 40 Minutes

Serves: 12

Ingredients:
- 5 Slices Bacon, Cooked & Crumbled

- 1½ Cups Sour Cream

- 1 Cup Cream Cheese

- 1 Cup Cheddar Cheese, Shredded

- 1 Cup Scallions, Sliced

Directions:

1. Start by heating your oven to 400 degrees F (200 degrees C).

2. Combine all of your ingredients together in a bowl, and then spoon out onto a baking dish.

3. Cook for 25 to 35 minutes. The cheese should be bubbling when it's done.

4. Let it cool slightly before serving.

Nutritional Information:
Total Carbs: 3.5 g
Protein: 6.58 g

Total Fat: 16.76 g
Calories: 190

Supreme Sausage Pizza Bomb

Prep Time: 5-10 Minutes

Total Time: 15-25 Minutes

Serves: 6

Ingredients:
- 12 Italian Sausage Slices

- 8 Black Olives, Pitted

- ¾ Cup Cream Cheese

- 2 Tablespoons Basil, Fresh & Chopped

- 6 Cherry Tomatoes

- Salt to Taste

Directions:

1. Dice your olives and Italian sausage slices.

2. Mix tomatoes, basil and cream cheese together until thoroughly blended.

3. Add your sausage slices and olives into your cream cheese, and then mix thoroughly.

4. Form into balls, and garnish with more basil and olives if desired.

Nutritional Information:
Total Carbs: 1.92 g
Protein: 3.29 g
Total Fat: 11.26 g
Calories: 120

Garlic Coconut Parmesan Chips

Prep Time: 5 Minutes

Total Time: 15-20 Minutes

Serves: 10

Ingredients:
- 1 Cup Parmesan Cheese, Grated

- 4 Tablespoons Coconut Flour

- 1 Teaspoon Rosemary

- ½ Teaspoon Garlic Powder

- ½ Teaspoon Basil

Directions:

1. Start by heating your oven to 350 degrees F (180 degrees C), and then take your Parmesan and flour, mixing it together. Make sure that you use grated Parmesan cheese instead of powdery Parmesan cheese or it'll all start to fall apart.

2. Add your herbs and continue to mix everything together.

3. Line a large baking sheet with parchment paper. Spoon mixture 2 inches apart on prepared baking sheet.

4. Bake for 8-10 minutes or until crisp and golden.

5. Let cool and enjoy!

Nutritional Information
Total Carbs: 1.76 g
Protein: 2.9 g
Total Fat: 2.8 g
Calories: 44

Dijon Mustard Cashew Sausage Ham

Prep Time: 5-10 Minutes

Total Time: 25 Minutes

Serves: 12

Ingredients:
- 3 Slices Pork Ham, Chopped

- 6 Ounces Sausage

- 6 Ounces Cream Cheese, Softened

- ¼ Cup Cashews, Chopped

- 1 Teaspoon Dijon Mustard

Directions:

1. Chop your sausages and pop them in the blender with your cashews, blending until smooth.

2. Beat the cream cheese and mustard together until smooth.

3. Roll your sausage mixture into balls and then form a cream cheese layer over it with your fingers. It should make about twelve balls.

4. Refrigerate them until firm, and then roll each ball in the chopped smoke pork ham before serving.

Nutrition Facts per Serving:
Total Carbs: 3.63 g
Protein: 9.03 g
Total Fat: 12.33 g
Calories: 159

Egg & Cheesy Fat Bombs

Prep Time: 5-10 Minutes

Total Time: 15-20 Minutes

Serves: 6

Nut Free, Sweetener Free

Ingredients: 2
Eggs, Boiled and Chopped

¼ Cup Butter

1 Cup Cream Cheese

½ Cup Blue Cheese, Grated

Directions:

1. Mix cream cheese, grated blue cheese, and butter in a medium mixing bowl.

2. Add in eggs, and continue to stir, making sure it's mixed well.

3. Make six balls, and then place them on parchment paper. Refrigerate for about 2 hours.

Nutritional Information:
Total Carbs: 1.85 g
Protein: 7.65 g
Total Fat: 21.58 g
Calories: 231

Delicious Olive Pesto Bombs

Prep Time: 5 Minutes

Total Time: 15 Minutes

Serves: 4

Ingredients:
- ½ Cup Cream Cheese

- ¼ Cup Pesto Sauce

- 6 Black Olives, Chopped

Directions:

1. Soften your cream cheese slightly, and then add the other two ingredients into the bowl, mixing completely.

2. Pour it into mini muffin cups, and then refrigerate.

Nutritional Information:

Total Carbs: 1.82 grams
Protein: 3.68 grams
Total Fat: 17.7 grams
Calories: 177

Prosciutto Avocado Fat Bombs

Prep Time: 10 Minutes

Total Time: 10 Minutes

Serves: 10

Ingredients:

- 1 Avocado

- 1 Lime

- 10 Slices Prosciutto

Directions:

1.   Halve your avocado, remove the seed, and then cut it into large slices.

2.	Squeeze lime over avocado slices, and then lay each prosciutto slice on a plate.

3.	Place each avocado slice on each prosciutto slice, squeeze a little bit more lime, and roll the prosciutto slice up.

Nutritional Information:
Total Carbs: 2.5 g
Protein: 2.9 gf

Total Fat: 4.5 g
Calories: 60

Cheesy Garlic & Lemon Fat Bombs

Prep Time: 5 Minutes

Total Time: 10 Minutes

Serves: 12

Ingredients:
- ¾ Cup Butter

- 4 Ounces Cream Cheese

- 1½ Lemon

- ¼ Cup Fresh Garlic, Minced

Directions:

1.   Soften butter and cream cheese, and then blend them with the lemon juice and garlic. Continue to blend until thoroughly mixed and fluffy.

2.   Make small balls using an ice cream scooper on a plate and refrigerate for at least 1 hour before serving.

Nutritional Information:
Total Carbs: 1.68 g
Protein: 1.33 g
Total Fat: 10.45 g
Calories: 105

Thick Cut Bacon Cheese Sticks

Prep Time: 5 Minutes

Total Time: 15 Minutes

Serves: 4

Ingredients:
- 4 Slices Bacon

- 4 Frigo Strings of Cheese (Emmental cheese is a great addition)

Directions:
1. Preheat the oven to 350 degrees F (180 degrees C).

2. Wrap cheese sticks with bacon and secure it together with a toothpick.

3. Bake in the oven for 8-10 minutes.

4. Remove and place on a paper towel to drain while cooling.

Nutritional Information:
Total Carbs: 0.42 g
Protein: 6.86 g
Total Fat: 15.3 g
Calories: 167

Bacon Herb Cream Cheese
Make this fat bomb and get all necessary nutrients in the appropriate portions.

Makes: 2 servings Prep Time: 30 min

Ingredients

1 cup of kefir cream cheese / yogurt cream cheese 2 cloves of garlic 1/2 cup of bacon fat, room temperature 1/4 cup of bacon bits 1/2 cup of Parmesan cheese, grated 1 tsp of fresh oregano, chopped Salt and fresh cracked pepper

Directions

1. Add cream cheese to your food processor. Run processor so as to loosen up cream cheese.
2. Add the garlic cloves and salt and pepper then run your food processor.
3. Pour some thin stream of the liquid bacon fat solely through hole in top of food processor, until well fully incorporated.
4. Place contents of food processor into the bowl.
5. Add remaining ingredients then fold into mixture. Divide this into 6 smaller portions then refrigerate.

Nutritional information per serving:

89 Calories,

10g Fat, trace g

Protein,

1g Carbohydrate,

trace g Dietary Fiber,

1g Effective Carbs

Low Carb Chocolate BonBons

Make this fat bombs full of healthy fats.

Makes: 6 servings Prep Time: 1 hr. 30 min

Ingredients

5 tablespoons of butter

3 tablespoons of coconut oil

2 tablespoons of cocoa powder

2 tablespoons of sugar-free raspberry syrup

Directions

1. Combine all the ingredients in a sauce pan placed over low heat until the chocolate sauce consistency.
2. Pour into the mold then freeze for about 2 hours.
3. Once frozen, just pop out of the mold then enjoy.

Nutritional information per serving:

100 calories,

0 NET carbs,

1 carbs,

10 grams of fat,

1 grams of protein and 1 grams of fiber

Cheesy Jalapeno Fat Bombs

Make this delicious fat bomb to help you boost your intake for fats.

Makes: 2 servings Prep Time: 10 min Cook Time 30 min

Ingredients

1/4 cup of unsalted butter or a ghee at room temperature 3.5 ounces of full-fat cream cheese 4 slices of bacon 1/4 cup of grated Gruyère cheese or a Cheddar cheese 2 g jalapeño of finely chopped peppers halved and seeded

Directions

1. In some bowl, mash together cream cheese and the butter or ghee, or just process in your food processor until they are smooth.
2. Preheat oven up to 325°F.
3. Line rimmed baking sheet with a parchment paper.
4. Lay bacon slices flat on parchment
5. *Place your sheet in preheated oven then cook for about 25 to 30 minutes.*
6. *Remove from oven and set aside to cool. Once cool, crumble bacon into the bowl then set aside.*
7. To cream cheese and the butter mixture, just add Gruyère or the Cheddar cheese, the jalapeños, and the bacon grease then mix well so as to combine. Refrigerate for about 1 hour.
8. Divide your mixture into some 6 fat bombs then place them on parchment-lined plate.

Nutritional information per serving:

Calories 142,

Total Fat 15g,

Total Carbs 0.9g,

Protein 3.5g

Chocolate Peanut Butter Fat Bomb

Make this chocolate and peanut butter fat bomb and get a very nice snack.

Makes: 12 fat bombs Prep Time 1 min Cook Time 10 min

Ingredients

1/4 cup of sugar free peanut butter

1/4 cup of coconut oil

1 ounce of unsweetened baking chocolate

1 tablespoon of cocoa

1/2 teaspoon of vanilla stevia drops

Directions

1. Completely melt the peanut butter, baking chocolate, coconut oil, and the cocoa in a chocolate melter or a double boiler.
2. Remove from the heat then stir in the stevia.
3. Pour into the silicone molds.
4. Freeze until hardened.
5. Remove from the molds. Store in an airtight container kept in a freezer.

Nutritional information per serving:

Calories 88,

Total Fat 8.7g,

Sodium 22mg,

Total Carbs 2.2g,

Protein 1.7g

White Chocolate Fat Bomb

Try this easy-to-make fat bomb featuring only 3 basic ingredients.

Makes: 8 servings Prep Time 5 min Cook Time 10 min

Ingredients

1/4 cup of cocoa butter

1/4 cup of coconut oil

10 drops of vanilla stevia drops

Directions

1. Melt together the cocoa butter and the coconut oil placed over low heat or kept in a double boiler.
2. Remove from the heat then stir in some vanilla flavored stevia drops.

3. Pour into the molds.
4. Chill until hardened.
5. Remove from the molds then keep stored in a refrigerator.

Nutritional information per serving:

125 calories,

0g carbs,

10g fat,

0g protein

Peanut Butter Chips

These peanut butter chips are sugar free, hence the best after a meal
Makes: 2 servings Prep Time 15 min Total Time 15 min

Ingredients

100 grams of cocoa butter melted

1/2 teaspoon of sea salt

1/4 cups of unsweetened peanut butter powder

1/3 cup of Natvia powder

Directions

1. Powder granular sweetener in some NutriBullet type blender or your then set aside.
2. Melt the cocoa butter with some sea salt in a chocolate melter, or microwave.
3. Stir in the peanut butter powder, the powdered sweetener, and the sea salt until they are well combined.
4. Spread the mixture out on the parchment paper, a silicone mat, or a shallow baking pan lined using plastic wrap placed over little water.
5. *If you need, cover using a parchment paper and smooth out the top with hand.*
6. *Place in a freezer for 30 minutes.*
7. Remove peanut butter sheet from the pan then cut into small chunks.

Nutritional information per serving:

52 calories,

8mg sodium,

3.7g fat,

3.2g carbs,

1.0g erythritol,

1.1g fiber,

4.4g protein,

1.1g net carbs

Chocolate Kisses Molded Candy

Make these sugar-free candies and enjoy with your family.

Makes: 42 kisses Prep Time 15 min Cook Time 15 min

Ingredients

4 oz. of unsweetened baking chocolate

1 oz. of cocoa butter food grade

3 tablespoons of Swerve Confectioners or the Sukrin Melis

1/8 teaspoon of stevia concentrated powder

1/2 teaspoon of vanilla extract

Directions

1. Melt the baking chocolate, the cocoa butter, and the powdered sweetener over a low heat or a double boiler until they are melted completely.
2. Remove the chocolate from the heat then stir in the stevia and the vanilla extracts.
3. Pour the melted chocolate into the molds. Refrigerate or freeze well until completely set.
4. Remove the chocolate from the molds and enjoy!

Nutritional information per serving:

Calories 20,

Total Fat 2.1g,

Sodium 1mg,

Total Carbs 0.8g,

Protein 0.3g

White Chocolate Bars

Make these sugar free chocolate bars and enjoy their delicacy.

Makes: 6 servings Prep Time 5 min Cook Time 10 min

Ingredients

3 tablespoons of Swerve Confectioners

2.5 ounces of cocoa butter food grade food grade

1 tablespoon of coconut milk powder 1 teaspoon of sunflower lecithin (optional) 1/8 teaspoon of stevia concentrated powder 1/8 teaspoon of monk fruit powder 1/2 teaspoon of vanilla extract

Directions

1. Melt together the cocoa butter, coconut milk powder, Swerve, stevia, lecithin and monk fruit in a microwave or chocolate melter.
2. Remove from the heat then stir in the vanilla.

3. Pour into the molds
4. Refrigerate until solid then remove from the mold.
5. Store covered in a refrigerator.

Nutritional information per serving:

Calories 123,

Total Fat 13.2g,

Cholesterol 0mg, Sodium

4mg,

Total Carbs 0.6g,

Protein og

Baked Pecan Prosciutto and Brie Savory Fat Bomb

Make this fat bomb as a show of love to your family.

Makes: 1 serving Prep time: 5 min Cook time: 12 min

Ingredients

1 slice of prosciutto

1 ounce of full-fat Brie cheese

6 pecan halves

⅛ Teaspoon of black pepper

Directions

1. Preheat the oven up to 350°F.
2. Take a slice of prosciutto then fold it into half to become almost square.
3. Place it in hole of muffin tin so as to line it up completely.
4. Chop Brie into little cubes, while leaving white skin on. Put Brie in prosciutto-lined cup.
5. *Stick pecan halves in the Brie.*
6. *Bake for 12 minutes, until the Brie becomes melted and the prosciutto is cooked.*
7. Cool for about 10 minutes before you can remove from muffin pan.

Nutritional information per serving:

Calories 183,

Fats 16.50g,

Fiber 1g,

Protein 8.42g

Coconut Oil Fat Bombs

Make these fat bombs which will melt in your mouth and enjoy their delicacy.

Make: 12 servings Prep Time: 15 min Cook Time: 5 min

Ingredients

2 cups of shredded unsweetened coconut

1/3 cup of coconut oil, melted

2 T of raw honey

4 ounces of raw dark chocolate chips

1/2 t of vanilla bean powder, optional

Directions

1. In a blender, add the coconut oil, raw honey, shredded coconut and the vanilla bean powder then blend well until the mixture becomes fine and crumbled.
2. Line small baking sheet or a plate with a wax paper. By use of a tablespoon-size measuring spoon, just scoop the mixture then form into some small mounds by use of your hands. Set on the wax paper. Put in a freezer for 10 minutes to set.

3. By use of a double boiler, just melt the chocolate until smooth. By use of a butter knife, drizzle the coconut bombs with the chocolate. Put back into the refrigerator so as to set for 10 minutes. Store in a refrigerator.

Nutritional information per serving:

Calories 123,

Total Fat 13.2g,

Cholesterol 0mg, Sodium

4mg,

Total Carbs 0.6g,

Protein 0g

Beef Machaca Keto Muffins

Make these muffins and enjoy them during your breakfast.

Makes: 8 muffins Prep time: 10 min Cook time: 30 min

Ingredients

2 tablespoons steak drippings, or the bacon drippings

½ cup of Beef Jerky Machaca

4 organic eggs

½ cup of roasted tomatillo salsa

½ cup of almond flour

Directions

1. Preheat the oven up to 350 degrees.
2. In your 7" nonstick ceramic pan placed on a medium heat, just melt fat of choice then add machaca to it.
3. Stir for 3 minutes or for the machaca to soften and fragrant.
4. Allow to cool for about 5 minutes.
5. *In food processor, just add eggs, almond flour, tomatillo salsa and machaca.*
6. *Mix on low for 30 seconds, or until all the ingredients become well blended.*
7. Pour the mixture into some 8 silicone muffin cups, or into silicone muffin mold.
8. Bake for 30 minutes at 350 degrees or until the toothpick becomes clean when it has been inserted in to muffin.

Nutritional information per serving:

Calories 128,

Fat 10g,

Fiber 0.75g,

Protein 6.6g

Sesame Keto Buns

Make these fat bombs good for you if you on a ketogenic diet.

Makes: 12 buns Prep time: 15 min Cook time: 50 min

Ingredients

1 cup of coconut flour

½ cup of sesame seeds and

½ cup for covering the buns

½ cup of pumpkin seeds

½ cup of psyllium powder

1 cup of hot water

1 tbs of Celtic sea salt

1 tbs of baking powder

8 egg whites

Directions

1. Preheat your oven up to 350 degrees.
2. Combine all the dry ingredients in the large bowl.
3. Mix well.
4. In some blender, blend egg whites until they are very foamy.
5. *Add foamy egg whites to dry ingredients then mix well using a spoon, or in food processor.*
6. *The dough will still be crumbly.*
7. Add 1 cup of the boiling water to mix then keep stirring until the smoother dough forms.

8. The dough will remain to be crumbly but it will stick when formed into bun.
9. Press the buns into the plate where the ½ cup of the sesame seeds was poured, so seeds will stick to top.
10. Place some sheet of the parchment paper on the cookie sheet.
11. Place the buns on paper.
12. Bake for 50 minutes at 350
13. Let cool inside oven for an extra crunchy top.
14. Makes 12 small buns

Nutritional information per serving:

Calories 133,

Fat 6.5g,

Fiber 9.5g,

Protein 6.9g

Cookie Dough Fat Bombs
Make these cookie dough fat bombs and get all the essential fats.

Makes: 10 servings Prep Time: 5 min

Ingredients

1/2 cup of coconut oil, melted

1/4 cup of almond Yum butter or the almond butter

1 tablespoon of maple syrup or some

10 drops of liquid stevia

3/4 cup of almond flour

1/4 cup of dark chocolate, finely chopped

Directions

1. In some bowl, combine almond butter, coconut oil, maple syrup, almond flour then mix well.
2. Fold in the chocolate.

3. Transfer to loaf pan then freeze until set.
4. Cut into squares then store in airtight container kept in the fridge.

Nutritional information per serving:

Calories: 209,

Fat: 19.9 g,

 Unsaturated fat: 9g,

Saturated fat: 10.9 g,

Trans fat: 0 g,

Sugar: 3.7 g,

Carbohydrates: 6.7 g,

Sodium: 4 mg

Fiber: 1.3 g,

Cholesterol: 1 mg,

Protein: 3.4 g

Bacon Wrapped Mozzarella Sticks

Try this recipe and get the best sticks for your breakfast.

Makes: 2 servings Prep time: 10 min Cook time: 3 min

Ingredients

1 Frigo of cheese heads cheese stick,

mozzarella 2 slices bacon Coconut oil Low sugar pizza sauce(optional) Toothpicks

Directions

1. Preheat the coconut oil in deep fryer up to 350 degrees.
2. Wrap your cut into half cheese sticks and bacon, while overlapping them.

3. Drop the bacon already wrapped with cheese in hot oil then cook until bacon becomes quite brown.
4. Remove to paper towel so as to cool for few minutes. Remove toothpick then enjoy with favorite dipping sauce!

Nutritional information per serving:

Calories: 103,

Fat: 9g,

Carbohydrates: 1g,

Fiber: 0g,

Protein: 7g

Breakfast Bacon Fat Bombs

Make these bacon fat bombs and enjoy them during your breakfast.

Makes: 6 servings Prep time: 30 min Cook Time: 20 min

Ingredients

1 Large Hardboiled Egg

¼ Avocado

4 tbsps. of Unsalted or Clarified Butter

1 tbsp. of Mayonnaise

1 seeded and diced Serrano Pepper

1 tbsp. of Cilantro, chopped Kosher Salt Cracked Pepper Juice of

¼ Lime

2 tbsps. of Bacon Grease

6 Bacon Slices, Cooked

Directions

1. In some large bowl, combine avocado, butter, hardboiled egg, mayonnaise cilantro and serrano pepper. Mash into smooth paste using a fork or a potato smasher. Season using salt and pepper, and add lime juice and stir.
2. Prepare the bacon in favorite fashion until it becomes crispy, while reserving 2 tablespoons bacon grease. Add bacon grease to fat bomb mixture then stir gently. Cover then place in a fridge for about 30 minutes, or until your mixture is cooled and can be formed into solid balls. Crumble bacon into some small bits in some small bowl.

3. Use a spoon to scoop out 6 amounts of fat bomb mixture then form into balls. Just add balls to bacon bits then roll around until they are completely covered.
4. Serve immediately.

Nutritional information per serving:

Calories: 103,

Fat: 9g,

Carbohydrates: 1g,

Fiber: 0g,

Protein: 7g

Amaretto Chilled Coffee

Try this delightful drink and enjoy it in a summer evening.

Makes: 2 fat bombs Prep Time: 8 min

Ingredients

2 cups of cooled brewed coffee

4 teaspoons of erythritol or granular Swerve /3 drops of stevia glycerite, divided 4 drops of divided amaretto flavor ½ cup of chilled heavy cream

1 teaspoon crumbled roasted almonds

Directions

1. Pour coffee into some medium bowl then mix with half of sweetener and half of amaretto flavor.
2. In your blender add the chilled cream, the remaining amaretto flavor, and the remaining sweetener, then blend on high till the cream is whipped.

3. Once it is ready to serve, just pour the coffee mix over the ice in 2 glasses.
4. Spoon the whipped cream on the top of coffee mix. Decorate using chopped almonds.
5. Serve immediately using a spoon and straw.

Nutritional information per serving:

Calories: 421,

Fat: 23g,

Protein: 12g,

Sodium: 55mg,

Fiber: 0g,

Carbohydrates: 45g,

Sugar: 0g

Coconut Coffee

Make this liquid fat bomb and enjoy it in the morning.

Makes: 1 fat bomb Prep Time: 1 min

Ingredients

1½ cups of hot brewed coffee

2 teaspoons of erythritol or granular of Swerve, or 2 drops of stevia glycerite

1 tablespoon of coconut oil

1 tablespoon of butter

1⁄8 teaspoon of sea salt

Directions

1. Place all the ingredients in some blender.

2. Blend on high for about 15 seconds.

3. Serve immediately.

Nutritional information per serving:

Calories: 534,

Fat: 28g,

Protein: 16g,

Sodium: 344mg,

Fiber: 0g,

Carbohydrates: 61g,

Sugar: 0g

Caffeine-Free Coconut Vanilla Tea

Try this hot drink for your breakfast and get all the fats essential for a healthy living.

Makes: 1 serving Prep Time: 2 min Cook Time: 8 min

Ingredients

1⁄2 cups of hot water

1 teabag of rooibos tea

1 teaspoons of erythritol or granular of Swerve, or 2 drops of stevia glycerite

1 tablespoon of coconut oil

1/8 teaspoon of vanilla extract (optional)

Directions

1. Place a teabag in water then brew for about 8 minutes.
2. Place the brewed tea in your blender with the remaining ingredients.
3. Blend on high for 15 seconds.
4. Serve immediately.

Nutritional information per serving:

Calories: 135,

Fat: 14g,

Protein: 0g,

Sodium: 11mg,

Fiber: 0g,

Carbohydrates: 8g,

Sugar: 0g

Creamy Mexican Hot Chocolate

Make this sugar-free drink and your family will enjoy it.

Makes: 2 servings Prep Time: 3 min Cook Time: 5 min

Ingredients

1/8 teaspoon of vanilla extract

4 tablespoons of unsweetened whipped cream

1/3 cup of cocoa powder

1 teaspoon of cinnamon

1 cup of water

1 cup of heavy cream

2 teaspoons of erythritol or granular of Swerve, or 2 drops

of stevia glycerite

Directions

1. In some small saucepan placed over very low heat, just combine all the ingredients except the whipped cream.
2. Heat while stirring frequently until the cocoa powder is dissolved completely, for about 5 minutes. Avoid boiling.

3. When it's ready to serve, just pour the chocolate into 2 cups then top with the whipped cream.

Nutritional information per serving:

Calories: 538,

Fat: 56g,

Protein: 6g,

Sodium: 63mg,

Fiber: 5g,

Carbohydrates: 17g,

Sugar: 0g

Po Cha

Make this drink and get a high-fat treat to get your day started.

Makes: 2 servings Prep Time: 3 min Cook Time: 8 min

Ingredients

4 cups of water

2 tablespoons of black tea leaves

2 tablespoons of butter

2 tablespoons of heavy cream

1/8 teaspoon of sea salt

1 drop of smoke flavor

Directions

1. In some small saucepan placed over high heat, just bring some water to a boil, and lower the heat to low.
2. Add some tea leaves to the water then simmer for about 3 minutes and strain.
3. Combine the brewed tea with the remaining ingredients in blender then mix on high for about 3 minutes.
4. Serve immediately.

Nutritional information per serving:

Calories: 153,

Fat: 17g, Protein:

0g, Sodium:

169mg,

Fiber: 0g,

Carbohydrates: 0g,

Sugar: 0g

Thai Iced Coffee
Try this version of Thai coffee and get every beneficial fat.

Ingredients

4 cups of cooled strong brewed coffee 4 teaspoons of erythritol or granular of Swerve, or 3 drops of stevia glycerite 2 tablespoons of coconut milk 1/8 teaspoon of vanilla extract 4 tablespoons of heavy cream

Directions

1. Pour the coffee into some large bowl then mix with coconut milk, sweetener and vanilla.
2. Pour the coffee mixture over the ice in some 2 tall glasses.
3. Pour the cream on the top of the coffee without stirring for the layers to remain separate.
4. Serve immediately using some tall spoon and straw.

Nutritional information per serving:

Calories: 548, Fat: 15g, Protein: 22g, Sodium: 77mg, Fiber: 0g, Carbohydrates: 80g, Sugar: 0g

Thai Iced Tea
Make this fat bomb drink during any time of the year.

Makes: 2 fat bombs Prep Time: 15 min Cook Time: 8 min

Ingredients

4 cups of water 2 tablespoons of black tea leaves, Ceylon variety 2 crushed cardamom pods 1 teaspoon of star anise seeds 1 teaspoons of erythritol or granular of Swerve, or 2 drops of stevia glycerite

1 tablespoons of heavy cream

2 tablespoons of coconut milk

1/8 teaspoon of vanilla extract

Directions

1. In some small saucepan placed over high heat, bring some water to boil, and lower the heat to low.
2. Add cardamom, tea leaves and the anise seeds then simmer for 3 minutes. Strain.
3. Let the brewed tea to cool, and pour over the ice in some 2 tall glasses.
4. In some small bowl combine cream, coconut milk, sweetener and the vanilla then stir well until the sweetener has dissolved.
5. *Pour the cream mix on the top of the tea without stirring for the layers to remain separate.*
6. Serve immediately with tall spoon and straw.

Nutritional information per serving:

Calories: 144,

Fat: 15g,

Protein: 1g,

Sodium: 28mg,

Fiber: 1g,

Carbohydrates: 7g,

Sugar: 0g

Blueberry Chocolate Smoothie

Try this drink with blueberries covered with chocolate and enjoy its flavor.

Makes: 1 serving Prep Time: 5 min

Ingredients

½ (13.5-ounce) can of coconut milk

1 tablespoon of powdered unflavored gelatin

 1 tablespoon of coconut oil, softened 1

tablespoons of cocoa powder

¼ cup of frozen blueberries 6 drops of liquid stevia

6 ice cubes

Directions

1. Pour milk and the gelatin into your blender then blend so as to combine.
2. Add the remaining ingredients other than ice cubes then blend for another minute until it is well mixed.
3. Place the ice cubes into a blender then process until the smoothie thickens.
4. Serve immediately.

Nutritional information per serving:

Calories: 560,

Fat: 55g,

Protein: 12g,

Sodium: 41mg,

Fiber: 5g, Carbohydrates: 16g, Sugar: 3g

Cinnamon Roll Smoothie

Make this high-fat drink and enjoy it.

Makes: 1 fat bomb Prep Time: 5 min

Ingredients

6 ounces of half-and-half

1 tablespoon of softened cream cheese

1 teaspoon of vanilla extract

½ teaspoon and ⅛ teaspoon of cinnamon, divided

6 drops of liquid stevia

6 ice cubes

Directions

1. Pour half-and-half and the cream cheese into some blender then blend to combine.
2. Add ½ teaspoon cinnamon, vanilla and stevia then blend for another minute until they are well mixed.
3. Place the ice cubes into a blender then process until the smoothie thickens.
4. Sprinkle ⅛ teaspoon of cinnamon on the top and serve.

Nutritional information per serving:

Calories: 283,

Fat: 24g,

Protein: 6g,

Sodium: 116mg,

Fiber: 1g,

Carbohydrates: 9g,

Sugar: 1g

Creamy Coconut Smoothie

Make this dairy-free smoothie and enjoy with your family.

Makes: 1 fat bomb Prep Time: 5 min **Ingredients**

½ (13.5-ounce) can of coconut milk

1 tablespoon of powdered unflavored gelatin

1 tablespoon of softened coconut oil

1 teaspoon of vanilla extract

1 tablespoon of unsweetened shredded coconut

6 drops of liquid stevia

6 ice cubes

Directions

1. Pour milk and the gelatin into the blender then blend so as to combine.
2. Add the remaining ingredients except the ice cubes and blend for another minute until they are well mixed.
3. Place the ice cubes into the blender then process until the smoothie thickens.
4. Serve immediately.

Nutritional information per serving:

Calories: 559,

Fat: 57g,

Protein: 10g,

Sodium: 41mg,

Fiber: 0g,

Carbohydrates: 7g,

Sugar: 1g

Eggnog Smoothie

Try this recipe and it will make an excellent fat bomb smoothie.

Makes: 2 fat bombs Prep Time: 10 min

Ingredients

2 large eggs, the yolk and the white separated

8 ounces of heavy cream

1/2 teaspoon of vanilla extract

1 teaspoon of nutmeg

1/8 teaspoon of ground cloves

3/8 teaspoon of cinnamon, divided

8 drops of liquid stevia

1 tablespoons of granular Swerve

8 ice cubes

Directions

1. In some medium bowl, beat the egg whites using a hand mixer until some stiff peaks form. Keep aside.
2. In some separate large bowl, beat the yolks using a mixer until the color changes to a pale yellow. Add vanilla,

   nutmeg, cream, cloves, 1/8 teaspoon cinnamon, the stevia, and the Swerve then stir well to combine.

3. Fold the whites into the yolk mixture.
4. Pour mix into the blender with the ice cubes then blend until the mixture thickens.
5. Sprinkle 1/8 teaspoon of cinnamon on the top of every glass then serve immediately.

Nutritional information per serving:

Calories: 468, Fat: 47g,

Protein: 9g, Sodium: 113mg,

Fiber: 1g, Carbohydrates: 5g,

Sugar: 1g

Gingerbread Gem Smoothie
Make this drink and enjoy the taste of ginger in it.

Makes: 1 fat bomb Prep Time: 5 min

Ingredients

6 ounces of unsweetened almond milk

1 tablespoon of powdered unflavored gelatin

1 tablespoon of almond butter

1/2 teaspoon of vanilla extract

1/2 teaspoon of ground ginger

1/2 teaspoon of cinnamon

6 drops of liquid stevia

6 ice cubes

Directions

1. Pour the milk and the gelatin into your blender then blend to combine.
2. Add the remaining ingredients except the ice cubes then blend for extra minute until they are well mixed.
3. Place the ice cubes into a blender then process until the smoothie thickens.
4. Serve immediately.

Nutritional information per serving:

Calories: 221, Fat: 11g,

Protein: 16g,

Sodium: 174mg,

Fiber: 3g,

Carbohydrates: 16g,

Sugar: 9g

Key Lime Pie Smoothie
Make this smoothie and enjoy its tropical taste.

Makes: 1 fat bomb Prep Time: 5 min

Ingredients

6 ounces of half-and-half

1 tablespoon of powdered unflavored gelatin

1 teaspoon of vanilla extract

2 tablespoons of freshly squeezed key lime juice

1 teaspoon of lime zest

6 drops of liquid stevia

6 ice cubes

Directions

1. Pour the half-and-half and the gelatin into some blender then blend so as to combine.
2. Add the remaining ingredients other than the ice cubes then blend for extra minute until they are well mixed.
3. Place the ice cubes into the blender then process until the smoothie thickens.
4. Serve immediately.

Nutritional information per serving:

Calories: 280,

Fat: 20g, Protein: 12g,

Sodium: 91mg,

Fiber: 2g,

Carbohydrates: 17g,

Sugar: 3g

Matcha Madness Smoothie

Make this smoothie which will provide you with some antioxidants.

Makes: 1 fat bomb Prep Time: 5 min **Ingredients**

½ (13.5-ounce) can of coconut milk

1 tablespoon of powdered unflavored gelatin

2 tablespoons of almond butter

1 teaspoon of vanilla extract

1 tablespoon of matcha

6 drops of liquid stevia Ice cubes

Directions

1. Pour milk and the gelatin into your blender then blend to combine.
2. Add the remaining ingredients other than the ice cubes then blend for extra minute until it is well mixed.
3. Place the ice cubes into a blender then process until the smoothie thickens.
4. Serve immediately.

Nutritional information per serving:

Calories: 610,

Fat: 57g,

Protein: 19g,

Sodium: 187mg,

Fiber: 4g,

Carbohydrates: 15g, Sugar: 4g

Orange Delight Smoothie

Make this smoothie with taste of creamsicle.

Ingredients

6 ounces of half-and-half Tablespoon of powdered unflavored gelatin

1 teaspoon of vanilla extract

2 tablespoons of orange juice,

freshly squeezed 1 teaspoon of orange zest

Drops of liquid stevia

6 ice cubes

Directions

1. Pour the half-and-half and the gelatin into your blender then blend to combine.
2. Add the remaining ingredients other than the ice cubes then blend for extra minute until they are well mixed.
3. Place the ice cubes into the blender then process until the smoothie thickens.
4. Serve immediately.

Nutritional information per serving:

Calories: 271,

Fat: 19g, Protein: 11g,

Sodium: 84mg,

Fiber: 0g,

Carbohydrates: 12g,

Sugar: 4g

Peanut Butter Cup Smoothie
Make this candy treat for your breakfast and enjoy.

Makes: 1 fat bomb Prep Time: 5 min **Ingredients**

½ (13.5-ounce) can of coconut milk

1 tablespoon of powdered unflavored gelatin

2 tablespoons of peanut butter

2 tablespoons of cocoa powder

1 teaspoon of vanilla extract

6 drops of liquid stevia

Ice cubes

Directions

1. Pour the milk and the gelatin into your blender then blend well to combine.
2. Add the remaining ingredients other than the ice cubes then blend for extra minute until they are well mixed.
3. Place the ice cubes into the blender then process until the smoothie thickens.
4. Serve immediately.

Nutritional information per serving:

Calories: 622,

Fat: 58g,

 Protein: 20g,

Sodium: 189mg,

Fiber: 6g, Carbohydrates: 18g,

Sugar: 4g

Po Cha (or Tibetan Butter Tea)

Make this tea and start your day with a high-fat treat.

Makes: 2 fat bombs Prep Time: 3 min Cook Time: 8 min

Ingredients

4 cups of water

2 tablespoons of black tea leaves

2 tablespoons of butter

2 tablespoons of heavy cream

1/8 teaspoon of sea salt Drop smoke of flavor

Directions

1. In some small saucepan placed over high heat, bring the water to boil, then lower the heat to low.
2. Add the tea leaves to the water then simmer for 3 minutes. Strain.

3. Combine the brewed tea with the remaining ingredients in some blender then mix on high for about 3 minutes.
4. Serve immediately.

Nutritional information per serving:

Calories: 153,

Fat: 17g,

Protein: 0g,

Sodium: 169mg,

Fiber: 0g,

Carbohydrates: 0g,

Sugar: 0g

Avocado Almond Smoothie

Try this recipe and make a creamy and nice smoothie and enjoy the taste of almond.

Makes: 2 fat bombs Prep Time: 3 min

Ingredients

½ pitted and peeled large avocado 1 cup of coconut milk ¼ cup of ice 1 teaspoon of almond extract 4 drops of liquid stevia 2 tablespoons of coconut butter

Directions

1. **Combine all the ingredients in a blender then blend until they are smooth.**
2. Serve immediately.

Nutritional information per serving: Calories: 423, Fat: 45g, Protein: 3g, Sodium: 18mg, Fiber: 3g, Carbohydrates: 7g, Sugar: 0g

Vanilla Smoothie

Make this smoothie and enjoy the taste of vanilla.

Makes: 1 fat bomb Prep Time: 5 min

Ingredients

6 ounces of half-and-half

1 tablespoon of powdered unflavored gelatin

1 teaspoon of vanilla extract

Pulp of 1 vanilla bean, scraped

4 drops of liquid stevia

6 ice cubes

Directions

1. Pour the half-and-half and the gelatin into your blender then blend to combine.
2. Add the remaining ingredients other than the ice cubes then blend for extra minute until they are well mixed.
3. Place the ice cubes into the blender then process until the smoothie thickens.
4. Serve immediately.

Nutritional information per serving:

Calories: 274,

Fat: 19g,

Protein: 11g,

Sodium: 83mg,

Fiber: 0g,

Carbohydrates: 8g,

Sugar: 1g

Vanilla Almond Butter Smoothie

Make this smoothie which features almond butter and enjoy its delicacy.

Makes: 1 fat bomb Prep Time: 5 min

Ingredients

6 ounces of unsweetened almond milk

1 tablespoon of powdered unflavored gelatin

2 tablespoons of almond butter

1 teaspoon of vanilla extract

1/4 teaspoon of almond extract (optional)

6 drops of liquid stevia

Ice cubes

Directions

1. Pour the milk and the gelatin into some blender then blend so as to combine.
2. Add the remaining ingredients other than the ice cubes then blend for extra minute until they are well mixed.
3. Place the ice cubes into the blender then process until the smoothie thickens.
4. Serve immediately.
5.

Nutritional information per serving:

Calories: 316,

Fat: 19g,

Protein: 19g,

Sodium: 248mg,

Fiber: 3g,

Carbohydrates: 17g,

Sugar: 10g

Vanilla Avocado Smoothie
Make this smoothie with a green color from the avocado.

Makes: 1 fat bomb Prep Time: 5 min **Ingredients**

½ (13.5-ounce) can of coconut milk

1 tablespoon of powdered unflavored gelatin

1 tablespoon of ground flaxseed

½ pitted and peeled medium avocado

1 teaspoon of vanilla extract

6 drops of liquid stevia

4 ice cubes

Directions

1. Pour gelatin, milk and flaxseed into the blender then blend to combine.
2. Add the remaining ingredients other than the ice cubes then blend for extra minute until they are well mixed.

3. Place the ice cubes into the blender then process until the smoothie thickens.
4. Serve immediately.

Nutritional information per serving:

Calories: 603,

Fat: 57g,

Protein: 14g,

Sodium: 46mg,

Fiber: 9g,

Carbohydrates: 17g,

Sugar: 1g

Strawberry Vanilla Smoothie
Make this smoothie and enjoy the sweet taste from the strawberries.

Makes: 1 fat bomb Prep Time: 5 min

Ingredients

½ (13.5-ounce) can of coconut milk Tablespoon of powdered unflavored gelatin

1 tablespoon of softened coconut oil

1 teaspoon of vanilla extract

¼ cup of chopped fresh strawberries

6 drops of liquid stevia

6 ice cubes

Directions

1. Pour the milk and the gelatin into the blender then blend to combine.
2. Add the remaining ingredients other than the ice cubes then blend for an extra minute until they are well mixed.
3. Place the ice cubes into the blender then process until the smoothie thickens.
4. Serve immediately.

Nutritional information per serving:

Calories: 540,

Fat: 54g,

Protein: 10g,

Sodium: 39mg,

Fiber: 1g,

Carbohydrates: 9g,

Sugar: 2g

Liquid Fat Bomb Smoothie
Make this smoothie full of healthy fats and enjoy!

Ingredients

1 cup of full fat coconut milk

1/4 cup of water

2 raw egg yolks

1 scoop of whey protein

2/3 cup of frozen berries

Directions

> 1. Add all the ingredients into your blender then blend well until smooth. Enjoy!

Nutritional information per serving:

Total Fat: 70 grams,

Saturated Fat: 50 grams,

Carbohydrate: 27 grams,

Protein: 27 grams,

Total Calories: 840

Keto Fat Bomb Smoothie
Make this healthy fat bomb in the shortest time possible.

Ingredients

1 Cup of Coconut Milk

2 tbsps. of Coconut Oil

1 tbsp. of Peanut Butter

1/2 tsp of Vanilla Extract

1/2 tsp of Cinnamon

1/2 Cup of Ice

Directions

1. Beginning with the ice, just add all the ingredients into your blender.
2. Blend well until smooth, then drink. You refrigerate for a later use, though you can have to remix ingredients using a spoon after settling.

Nutritional information per serving:

Calories 883,

Protein 9g,

Fat 79g,

Carbs 17g

Spiced Cocoa Coolers

Make this keto-friendly fat bomb and use it for snacking.

Makes: 10 servings Prep Time 1hr 30 min

Ingredients

1 cup of heavy whipping cream

2 tbsps. of unsweetened cocoa powder

1 vanilla bean

1 tsp of cinnamon

¼ tsp of cayenne pepper

2 tbsps. of Erythritol

15-20 drops of Stevia extract

Directions

1. Your ingredients will dissolve easily after warming up cream or the coconut milk slightly.
2. Place all other ingredients in cream then mix until combined well.

3. Pour your liquid into the ice-cube tray then transfer this into freezer for 1-2 hours. Enjoy!

Nutritional information per serving:

Total carbs 1.8g,

Fiber 0.7g,

Protein 0.7g,

Fat 5g

Chapter 5) Frozen Fat Bombs:

Mocha Vanilla Fat Bomb Pops

Make these fat bombs and enjoy them when frozen.

Makes: 6 servings Prep Time: 10 min

Ingredients

4 tbsps. of unsalted butter

2 tbsps. of heavy cream

1/2 tsp of vanilla extract

4 tbsps. of coconut oil

1/2 tbsp. of unsweetened cocoa powder

1/2 tsp of coffee extract Stevia, to taste

Directions

1. *Make vanilla layer:*
2. Soften butter in a microwave until liquefied.

3. Add the heavy cream then stir. Keep aside.
4. Once cooled, add in vanilla then blend well.

5. Pour vanilla mixture into the muffin liners/tins. Place into your refrigerator until it is firm.

Make mocha layer:

1. Mix coconut oil, coffee extract, cocoa powder and stevia.
2. Remove the vanilla layer from fridge then pour in mocha mixture, while filling the cups to top.
3. Add the popsicle sticks then freeze for 20 to 30 minutes.

Nutrition information per serving:

167 Calories; trace

Protein, 19g

Fat,.5g

Dietary Fiber, 1g Carbohydrate

Mocha Ice Bombs

Make these frozen fat bombs and they will help you overcome hunger.

Makes: 12 servings Prep Time: 10 min

Ingredients

Mocha Ice Bombs

1cup of cream cheese

1/4cupof powdered sweetener

2 tbsp. of unsweetened cocoa

1/4cup of strong coffee chilled Chocolate coating

70g of melted chocolate

28g of melted cocoa butter

Directions

1. Add coffee to cream cheese, the cocoa, and the sweetener.
2. Blend until smooth.

3. To make ice bomb shape, just roll 2 tablespoons of mocha ice bomb mixture then place them on a tray or a plate lined with a baking parchment.

Chocolate coating

1. Mix your melted chocolate and the cocoa butter together.
2. Roll every ice bomb in chocolate coating then place back on a lined tray/plate.

3. Place in a freezer for about 2 hours.

Nutritional information per serving:

Calories 127,

Total fat 12.9g,

Total carbs 2.2g,

Protein 1.9g

Coconut White Chocolate

This is the best fat bomb for you if you love coconut.

Makes: 12 fat bombs Prep Time: 3 hours Cook Time:

Ingredients

1/4 cup of coconut oil

1/4 cup of cocoa butter

1 tsp of vanilla extract

12 drops of liquid stevia

1 tsp of shredded coconut, unsweetened

Directions

1. Combine cocoa butter, coconut oil, vanilla, and the stevia in some small saucepan placed over medium heat, while stirring frequently until the ingredients have melted, then turn off heat.
2. Add coconut then stir well so as to combine.
3. Pour your mixture into the 12 molds of siliconebottomed ice cube tray or the silicone candy mold tray to be 3/4 full.
4. Freeze until it's set. Serve from a freezer.

Nutritional information per serving:

Calories: 82,

Fat: 9g,

Protein: 0g,

Frozen

5 minutes

Sodium: 0mg,

Fiber: 0g,

Carbohydrates: 0g,

Sugar: 0g

Almond Choco-Nut

Make this frozen fat bomb full of flavor and fats.

Makes: 12 fat bombs Prep Time: 3 hours Cook Time:

Ingredients

1/4 cup of coconut oil

1/4 cup of almond butter

12 drops of liquid stevia

2 tablespoons of cocoa powder

1/4 cup of almonds

1 tablespoon of shredded coconut

Directions

1. Combine almond butter, coconut oil and stevia in some small pot placed over medium heat, while stirring frequently until the ingredients have melted, then turn off heat.
2. Add the cocoa powder and the almonds then stir well so as to combine.
3. Pour the mixture into the 12 molds of ice cube tray or the silicone candy mold tray to be about 3/4 full.
4. Sprinkle the shredded coconut on the top of every fat bomb.
5. Freeze well until set. Serve from a freezer.

Nutritional information per serving:

Frozen

5 minutes

Calories: 87,

Fat: 8g,

Protein: 2g,

Sodium: 25mg,

Fiber: 1g,

Carbohydrates: 2g,

Sugar: 1g

Maca-Nutty Bites

Make these fat bombs and drench them in chocolate.

Makes: 12 fat bombs Prep Time: 3 hours Cook Time:

Ingredients

¼ cup of coconut oil

¼ cup of almond butter

1 tsp of vanilla extract

12 drops of liquid stevia

1 tbsp. of cocoa powder

12 whole macadamia nuts

Directions

1. Combine coconut oil, vanilla, almond butter and stevia in some small saucepan placed over medium heat, while stirring frequently till the ingredients melt. Turn off the heat.
2. Add the cocoa powder then stir well so as to combine.
3. Pour the mixture into 12 molds until each is about 2⁄3 full.
4. Place a macadamia nut into every filled mold.
5. Freeze until set, then serve from freezer.

Nutritional information per serving:

Calories: 93,

Fat: 9g

Frozen

5 minutes

Protein: 2g,

Sodium: 25mg,

Fiber: 1g,

Carbohydrates: 2g,

Sugar: 1g

Frozen Coffee Hazelnut Coconut

These fat bombs will make you enjoy the flavor of coffee.

Makes: 12 fat bombs Prep Time: 3 hours Cook Time: 5 minutes

Ingredients

¼ cup of coconut oil

¼ cup of almond butter

1 tsp of instant coffee granules 12

drops of liquid stevia

1 tablespoons of cocoa powder

12 hazelnuts

Directions

1. Combine almond butter, coffee, coconut oil and the stevia in some small saucepan placed over medium heat,

while stirring frequently until the ingredients melt. Turn off heat.

2. Add the cocoa powder then stir well so as to combine.

3. Pour the mixture into 12 molds for each to be about 2/3 full.

4. Place a hazelnut into every filled mold.

5. Freeze until set, then serve from freezer.

Nutritional information per serving:

Calories: 96,

Fat: 8g,

Protein: 2g,

Sodium: 25mg,

Fiber: 1g,

Carbohydrates: 2g,

Sugar: 1g

Frozen Butter Rum Chocolate

This is the best fat bomb for you if you like how run tastes.

Makes: 12 fat bombs Prep Time: 3 hours Cook Time: 5 minutes

Ingredients

1/4 cup of coconut oil

1/4 cup of almond butter

2 teaspoons of rum extract

12 drops of liquid stevia

2 tablespoons of cocoa powder

Directions

1. Combine all the ingredients other than cocoa powder in some small saucepan placed over medium heat, while stirring frequently until the ingredients melt. Turn off heat.
2. Add the cocoa powder then stir well so as to combine.
3. Pour the mixture into 12 molds until each is about 3/4 full.
4. Freeze until set then serve from freezer.

Nutritional information per serving:

Calories: 75,

Fat: 7g,

Protein: 2g,

Sodium: 25mg,

Fiber: 1g,

Carbohydrates: 2g,

Sugar: 1g

Frozen Salted Caramel Almond

Make these frozen fat bombs and enjoy the taste of butter and cream.

Makes: 12 fat bombs Prep Time: 3 hours Cook Time: 5 minutes

Ingredients

1/4 cup of butter

1/4 cup of granular Swerve

2 teaspoons of vanilla extract

12 whole almonds

1 teaspoon of coarse sea salt

Directions

1. Combine Swerve, butter and vanilla in some small saucepan placed over medium heat, while stirring frequently until the ingredients melt. Turn off heat.
2. Place 1 almond to each mold of 12-mold silicone candy tray.
3. Pour the mixture over every almond until the molds become about 3/4 full.
4. Sprinkle salt on the top of every fat bomb.
5. Freeze until set, then serve from freezer.

Nutritional information per serving:

Calories: 64,

Fat: 7g,

Protein: 0g,

Sodium: 296mg,

Fiber: 0g,

Carbohydrates: 1g,

Sugar: 0g

Frozen Orange Creamsicle
Try these fat bombs and use them as a daily snack.

Makes: 12 fat bombs Prep Time: 3 hours

Ingredients

¼ cup of coconut oil ¼ cup of heavy whipping cream 2 ounces of cream cheese, softened 2 tablespoons of orange juice 1 tablespoon of orange zest 12 drops of liquid stevia

Directions

1. Combine ingredients in some small wide-mouthed jar or in a bowl then blend with immersion blender, for about 30 seconds.
2. Spread the mixture into your 12 molds of silicone candy mold tray.
3. Freeze until set then serve from freezer.

Nutritional information per serving:

Calories: 75,

Fat: 8g,

Protein: 0g,

Sodium: 17mg,

Fiber: 0g,

Carbohydrates: 1g,

Sugar: 0g

Frozen Matcha Cream

Make these fat bombs and they will give you a big boost to your energy.

Makes: 12 fat bombs Prep Time: 3–12 hours Cook Time: 5 minutes

Ingredients

Ganache 3 ounces of cocoa butter

3 ounces of coconut cream

1 tablespoon of coconut oil

1/2 teaspoon of matcha

2 tablespoons of confectioners Swerve

2 drops of stevia glycerite

1/8 teaspoon of sea salt Coating

2 tablespoons of matcha

Directions

1. In some small double boiler placed over medium-low heat, just melt the cocoa butter as you stir slowly.
2. Add coconut cream, 1/2 teaspoon matcha, coconut oil, Swerve, the stevia, and the sea salt then mix well until they are incorporated.

3. Remove from the heat then continue stirring for about 10 seconds.
4. Pour into the silicone mold for the chocolate or the candy in desired shape.

5. Freeze for about 3 hours. Once frozen, remove the shapes from the molds and sprinkle with about 2 tablespoons of matcha so as to coat tops.

6. They may be stored in some sealed container in a freezer or a refrigerator.

Nutritional information per serving:

Calories: 103,

Fat: 9g,

Protein: 0g,

Sodium: 291mg,

Fiber: 0g,

Carbohydrates: 6g,

Sugar: 5g

Frozen Coconut Rum
These are good fat bombs for you while in a vacation.

Makes: 10 fat bombs Prep Time: 5 hours Cook Time: 5 min

Ingredients

Ganache 2 ounces of cocoa butter 2 ounces of coconut cream 2 tablespoons of confectioners Swerve 1/4 teaspoon of rum flavor 2 drops of stevia glycerite 4 tablespoons of unsweetened shredded coconut Coating 2 tablespoons of shredded coconut

Directions

1. In some small double boiler placed over medium-low heat, just melt the cocoa butter as you stir slowly.
2. Add Swerve, rum flavor, coconut cream, stevia, and some 4 tablespoons of shredded coconut then mix well until well incorporated.
3. Remove from the heat then keep on stirring for about 10 seconds.
4. Pour into the silicone mold for the chocolate or the candy in the desired shape.
5. Freeze for about 3 hours. Once frozen, just remove the ganache shapes from the molds then sprinkle using 2 tablespoons of shredded coconut so as to coat tops.

Nutritional information per serving:

Calories: 86,

Fat: 8g,

Protein: 0g,

Sodium: 3mg,

Fiber: 0g,

Carbohydrates: 5g,

Sugar: 5g

Almond Cookie Popsicles
Try these sweet fat bombs free of any dairy product.

Makes: 8 fat bombs Prep Time: 8–12 hours Cook Time: 0 minutes

Ingredients

1½ cups of coconut cream, chilled

½ cup of almond butter

1 teaspoon of vanilla extract

¼ cup of erythritol

Directions

1. Put all your ingredients in some blender then blend until they are mixed completely, about 30 seconds.
2. Pour the mix into the 8 Popsicle molds, while tapping the molds so as to dislodge the air bubbles.
3. Freeze for about 8 hours.
4. Remove the popsicles from the molds. If the popsicles become hard to be removed from the containers, run the molds under the hot water briefly then the popsicles will become loose.

Nutritional information per serving:

Calories: 294,

Fat: 17g,

Protein: 5g,

Sodium: 94mg,

Fiber: 1g,

Carbohydrates: 39g,

Sugar: 30g

Butter Pecan Popsicles

Make these fat bombs and they will cool you during the summer time.

Makes: 8 fat bombs Prep Time: 10 hours Cook Time: 5 minutes

Ingredients

2 tablespoons of butter

1 cup of coarsely chopped pecans

1 tablespoons of erythritol

1½ cups of heavy cream

1 teaspoon of vanilla extract

⅛ teaspoon of salt

Directions

1. In some medium nonstick pan placed over medium heat, just melt butter. Add pecans and a tablespoon of sweetener then cook for about 3 minutes, then keep aside to cool.
2. In some blender, mix the cream, 2 tablespoons of sweetener, vanilla, and the salt for about 10 seconds.
3. Scoop the cooled pecans into the bottom of the 8 Popsicle molds, while dividing them equally.
4. Pour the cream mix into the molds, while tapping the molds so as to dislodge the air bubbles.
5. *Freeze for about 8 hours.*
6. Remove the popsicles from the molds. If the popsicles become hard to dislodge from the containers, just run the molds under the hot water and the popsicles will become loose.

Nutritional information per serving:

Calories: 276,

Fat: 29g

Protein: 2g,

Sodium: 54mg,

Fiber: 1g,

Carbohydrates: 8g,

Sugar: 1g

Creamy Peanut Butter Popsicles

These are best fat bombs for you, featuring a combination of chocolate and peanut butter.

Makes: 8 fat bombs Prep Time: 10 hours Cook Time: 8 minutes

Ingredients

½ cup of mascarpone

½ cup of unsweetened peanut butter

1 Cup of heavy cream

1 tablespoons of erythritol or granular Swerve

1 teaspoon of vanilla extract

1 ounces of unsweetened baking chocolate

1 tablespoon of confectioners Swerve

Directions

1. In some small saucepan placed over low heat, just combine peanut butter, mascarpone and cream. Stir well until melted, for about 3 minutes. Keep aside to cool.
2. In some blender, add the cream mixture, the sweetener, and the vanilla. Blend well until combined, for about 10 seconds.

3. Pour the cream mix into your molds, while tapping the molds so as to dislodge the air bubbles.
4. Freeze for at least 8 hours.
5. *In some double boiler placed over medium-low heat, just melt the chocolate and the confectioners Swerve.*
6. *Remove the popsicles from your molds. If the popsicles become hard to be removed from containers, just run*

molds under the hot water briefly and the popsicles will become loose.

7. Use a spoon to drizzle the melted chocolate each Popsicle then serve immediately.

Nutritional information per serving:

Calories: 288,

Fat: 28g,

Protein: 6g,

Sodium: 134mg,

Fiber: 2g,

Carbohydrates: 11g,

Sugar: 3g

Coconut Vanilla Popsicles
Make these fat bombs and everyone in your family will love them.

Makes: 8 fat bombs Prep Time: 10 hours

Ingredients

2 cups of coconut cream, chilled

1/4 cup of unsweetened shredded coconut

1 teaspoon of vanilla extract

1/4 cup of erythritol or a granular Swerve

Directions

1. Place your ingredients in some blender then blend until they are mixed completely, for about 30 seconds.
2. Pour the mix into your 8 Popsicle molds, while tapping molds so as to dislodge the air bubbles.
3. Freeze for about 8 hours.
4. Remove the popsicles from your molds. If the popsicles become hard to be removed from the containers, just run the molds under hot water for the popsicles to become loose.

Nutritional information per serving:

Calories: 274,

Fat: 13g,

Protein: 1g,

Sodium: 27mg,

Fiber: 0g,

Carbohydrates: 46g,

Sugar: 38g

Dark Chocolate Popsicles

Try these fat bombs and enjoy the smooth and tasty flavor of dark chocolate.

Makes: 4 fat bombs Prep Time: 10 hours

Ingredients

½ cup of coconut cream

⅓ cup of cocoa powder

1 tablespoons of erythritol

1 medium pitted and peeled avocado

⅛ teaspoon of vanilla extract

⅛ teaspoon of salt

Directions

1. Place your ingredients in some small food processor or a blender then blend until mixed completely, for about 30 seconds.
2. Pour the mixture into 4 Popsicle molds, while tapping the molds so as to dislodge the air bubbles.
3. Freeze for about 8 hours.
4. Remove the popsicles from molds. In case the popsicles become hard to be removed from the containers, just run molds under the hot water for the popsicles to become loose.

Nutritional information per serving:

Calories: 229,

Fat: 14g,

Protein: 3g,

Sodium: 92mg,

Fiber: 6g,

Carbohydrates: 37g,

Sugar: 20g

Ginger Cream Popsicles

Make these fat bombs and get adequate supply of health fats.

Makes: 8 fat bombs Prep Time: 10 hours

Ingredients

2 cups of chilled coconut cream

2 tablespoons of coconut oil

1 teaspoon of ground ginger

¼ cup of erythritol or granular Swerve

Directions

1. Place all the ingredients in blender then blend until mixed completely, for about 30 seconds.
2. Pour the mixture into 8 Popsicle molds, while tapping the molds so as to dislodge the air bubbles.

3. Freeze for about 8 hours.
4. Remove the popsicles from the molds. In case the popsicles become hard to be removed from the containers, just run molds under the hot water for the popsicles to become loose.

Nutritional information per serving:

Calories: 295,

Fat: 15g,

Protein: 1g,

Sodium: 27mg,

Fiber: 0g,

Carbohydrates: 46g,

Sugar: 38g

Hazelnut Cappuccino Popsicles

Make these fat bombs for your summer days.

Makes: 8 fat bombs Prep Time: 10 hours Cook Time: 1 min

Ingredients

1 cup of heavy whipping cream

1/8 teaspoon of hazelnut flavor

1 cup of espresso or strong coffee

1/4 cup of erythritol or granular Swerve

1/2 cup of crumbled hazelnuts

Directions

1. Place all the ingredients other than hazelnuts in some blender then blend until mixed, for about 30 seconds.
2. Pour the mixture into 8 Popsicle molds, while tapping molds so as to dislodge the air bubbles.
3. Freeze for 8 hours.
4. In some small nonstick pan placed over medium heat, just toast the crumbled hazelnuts for about 1 minute, while stirring constantly.
5. Remove the popsicles from the molds. In case the popsicles become hard to be removed from the containers, just run molds under the hot water for the popsicles to become loose.
6. Before you can serve, press the popsicles into the hazelnut crumbles so that they can coat on the outside.

Nutritional information per serving:

Calories: 148,

Fat: 15g,

Protein: 2g,

Sodium: 11mg,

Fiber: 1g,

Carbohydrates: 8g,

Sugar: 0g

Matcha Popsicles

Try these fat bombs and enjoy the energizing effect of matcha.

Makes: 8 servings Prep Time: 10 hours

Ingredients

2 cups of chilled coconut cream

2 tablespoons of coconut oil

1 teaspoon of matcha

¼ cup of erythritol or granular Swerve

Directions

1. Place all the ingredients in your blender then blend until mixed completely, for about 30 seconds.
2. Pour the mixture into 8 the Popsicle molds, while tapping the molds so as to dislodge the air bubbles.
3. Freeze for 8 hours.
4. Remove the popsicles from the molds. In case the popsicles become hard to be removed from the containers, just run molds under the hot water for the popsicles to become loose.

Nutritional information per serving:

Calories: 294,

Fat: 15g,

Protein: 1g,

Sodium: 88mg,

Fiber: 0g,

Carbohydrates: 46g,

Sugar: 38g

Orange Chocolate Popsicles

Make these fat bombs and get the flavor of chocolate which will leave everyone smiling.

Makes: 4 fat bombs Prep Time: 10 hours

Ingredients

½ cup of coconut cream

½ cup of cocoa powder

1 tablespoons of erythritol or granular Swerve

1 teaspoon of orange zest

1 medium pitted and peeled avocado

⅛ teaspoon of orange extract

⅛ teaspoon of salt

Directions

1. Place all the ingredients in some small food processor or a blender then blend until mixed completely, for about 30 seconds.
2. Pour the mixture into 4 Popsicle molds, while tapping the molds so as to dislodge the air bubbles.
3. Freeze for 8 hours or overnight.
4. Remove the popsicles from the molds. In case the popsicles become hard to be removed from the containers, just run molds under the hot water for the popsicles to become loose.

Nutritional information per serving:

Calories: 237,

Fat: 15g,

Protein: 4g,

Sodium: 93mg, Fiber: 7g,

Carbohydrates: 36g,

Sugar: 20g

Mint Chocolate Chip Popsicles

Make these fat bombs and have everyone taste them.

Makes: 8 fat bombs Prep Time: 10 hours Cook Time: 5 min

Ingredients

2 cups of coconut cream

1 cup of fresh mint leaves

1 ounce of unsweetened chocolate chips

1/4 cup of erythritol or granular Swerve

Directions

1. Combine the coconut milk and the mint in some medium saucepan placed over medium heat.
2. Simmer until some bubbles begin to appear, for about 5 minutes.
3. Remove from the heat then allow to steep for 20 minutes.
4. Strain through some fine-mesh sieve into bowl.
5. *Add the chocolate and the sweetener then stir well.*
6. *Pour the mixture into 4 Popsicle molds, while tapping the molds so as to dislodge the air bubbles.*
4. Freeze for 8 hours or overnight.
5. Remove the popsicles from the molds. In case the popsicles become hard to be removed from the containers, just run molds under the hot water for the popsicles to become loose.

Nutritional information per serving:

Calories: 304,

Fat: 16g,

Protein: 2g,

Sodium: 32mg,

Fiber: 2g,

Carbohydrates: 48g,

Sugar: 38g

Fat Bomb Ice Cream

Try this creamy and dairy-free frozen fat bomb and enjoy its flavor.

Makes: 5 servings Prep Time: 10 min

Ingredients

4 pastured eggs, whole

4 yolks of pastured eggs

1/3 cup of melted cacao butter

1/3 cup of melted coconut oil

1/3 cup of xylitol

1/3 cup of flavor variation

¼ cup of MCT oil

2 tsp of vanilla bean powder

8-10 ice cubes

Directions

1. Add all the ingredients other than the ice cubes into a jug of high powdered blender. Blend this on high for about 2 minutes, or until creamy.
2. As the blender runs, remove top portion of lid then drop in ice cube, one at a time, while allowing your blender to run for about 10 seconds between every ice cube.

3. Once you have added all ice, pour your cold mixture into the ice cream maker then churn it on high for about 2030 minutes, based on the ice cream maker.

4. Serve this immediately as a soft-serve or scoop it into 9 * 5 loaf pan then freeze for about 45 minutes. Store while covered in freezer for about a week.

Nutritional information per serving:

Calories: 431,

Calories from

Fat: 399,

Saturated Fat: 34 g,

Total Fat: 44.3,

Sodium: 56 mg,

Carbs: 3.4 g,

Cholesterol: 299> mg,

Dietary Fiber: 1.6 g,

Protein: 7.7 g,

Net Carbs: 1.8 g

Valentine's Day Keto Fat Bombs

Make these frozen fat bombs for your sweetheart on the Valentine 's Day and enjoy their flavor.

Makes: 4 servings Prep time: 2 min Cook time: 2 min

Ingredients

2 Oz. of Coconut Oil

1 Oz. of Cream Cheese

½ Oz. of Torani Sugar Free Vanilla Syrup

1 teaspoon of Cocoa Powder

2 Oz of Dark Chocolate

8 Drops of EZ-Sweetz

2 Oz. of Almond Butter

Directions

1. Combine all items other than almond butter then microwave for about 30 seconds
2. Stir in ingredients and microwave again then keep on stirring if the chocolate fails to melt.
3. Pour the base layer into mold you are using
4. Then by use of a spoon, place some dollop of the Almond Butter at the center.
5. *Fill in the remaining mold to top*
6. *Freeze until your chocolate becomes hard, then hard push these out of mold*
7. Store in a fridge

Nutritional information per serving:

Calories 297,

Fat 30,

Carbs 7,

Fiber 3,

Protein 5

Frozen Chocolate Peanut Butter Cheesecake Bombs

Try these fat bombs and enjoy them in the shortest time possible.

Makes: 12 servings Prep Time: 1 hr.

Ingredients

6 oz. of Cream Cheese

1/3 cup of Natural Creamy Peanut Butter

2 tbsps. of Xylitol

1 tsp of Vanilla Extract

1 pinch of 1 cup of Heavy Cream

1/8 tbsp. of Xanthan Gum

3 bars of Double Chocolate Crunch Bar, Snack Caramel

Directions

1. Beat the softened cream cheese using a mixer placed on medium speed to become creamy. Add powdered granular sugar substitute, peanut butter, and vanilla then beat to combine. Taste then increase the sweetness if needed by adding some pinch of stevia.

2. Add 1 cup of cream and the 1/4 teaspoon of xanthan gum, beating until it becomes light and fluffy.

3. Cut the Atkins bars lengthwise to form three segments and finely chop segments. Fold into the mixture. By use of a 2 tablespoon scoop onto wax paper readily covered with a baking sheet.
4. Put in a freezer until frozen.

Nutritional information per serving:

Calories 208,

Protein 5.2g,

Fiber 5.3g,

Fat 18.3g

Ultimate Keto Ice-Cream

Try this recipe and you will get a creamy and soft ice-cream.

Makes: 8 servings Prep Time: 1 hr.

Ingredients

½ cup of extra virgin coconut oil

½ cup of butter

4 large of egg yolks

2 large of eggs

¼ cup of Erythritol

25-30 drops of Stevia extract

1 cup of coconut milk

2 vanilla beans

Directions

1. Separate egg yolks from the egg whites. Ensure butter and the coconut oil have been softened at room temperature.
2. Mix the coconut oil, butter, vanilla extract, the powdered Erythritol and the stevia together.
3. Slowly add egg yolks and the whole eggs as you blend one by one then process until they are smooth.
4. Pour in coconut milk then continue blending.
5. Scoop your mixture into ice-cream maker then process depending on manufacturer's instructions.
6. Remove from ice-cream maker when half-way made. Use immersion blender then pulse until smooth.
7. Return to the ice-cream maker and continue until your ice-cream is done. If you see lumps, pulse by use of an immersion blender. Eat immediately or just place in a freezer for 30-60 minutes. Enjoy!

Nutritional information per serving:

Total carbs 2.3g,

Fiber 06g,

Protein 3.6g,

Fat 34.6g,

Magnesium 15mg,

Potassium 94mg

7) Conclusion

The kind of food you eat has a great impact on your health. It is necessary that one eats the best diet which will help them live a healthy lifestyle.

A ketogenic diet is one of the best diets one can adhere to. It helps one maintain the right weight without having to starve themselves.

When it comes to limiting your carbohydrates, a good guideline to shoot for is to consume less than 15 net carb grams per day. To determine your net carbs, you simply add up how many carbohydrates you consumed in a 24-hour period and then subtract that number from the amount of fiber you consumed during that same amount of time.

Prior to making any major dietary changes you should always consult a healthcare professional or registered nutritionist to ensure that you aren't accidentally doing more harm to yourself then good. When it comes to sticking to the ketogenic diet, net carbohydrates should only make up 5 percent of your diet, 25 percent should be protein and the remaining 70 percent should be made up of healthy fats. Wheats and starches of all types should be off limits and most carbohydrates should come from nuts, vegetables and dairy products.

Dark, leafy green vegetables should be a staple of most meals as should several natural fats and a good source of protein. Consider meals such as chicken with vegetables coated with olive oil, or steak with roasted cauliflower slathered in butter.

Finally, if you enjoyed this book, then I would like to ask you for a favor, would you be kind enough to leave a review for this book on Amazon? It would be greatly appreciated!

Thank you and good luck!

Made in the USA
Middletown, DE
17 April 2018